FROM
DARKNESS
TO
LIGHT

OVERTURES TO BIBLICAL THEOLOGY

Editors

WALTER BRUEGGEMANN, Professor of Old Testament at Eden Theological Seminary, St. Louis, Missouri

JOHN R. DONAHUE, S.J., Professor of New Testament at the Jesuit School of Theology, Berkeley, California

Aspects
of
Conversion
in the
New Testament

FROM DARKNESS TO LIGHT

BEVERLY ROBERTS GAVENTA

FORTRESS PRESS   Philadelphia

Library of Congress Cataloging in Publication Data

Gaventa, Beverly Roberts.
From darkness to light.

(Overtures to biblical theology; 20)
Bibliography: p.
Includes index.
1. Conversion—Biblical teaching. 2. Bible.
N.T.—Criticism, interpretation, etc. I. Title.
II. Series.
BS2545.C59G38 1986   248.2'4   85–16309
ISBN 0–8006–1545–8

1817G85   Printed in the United States of America   1–1545

For my parents
Margaret Headrick Roberts
and
Harold Edward Roberts

Contents

Editor's Foreword

In his excellent bibliographical essay on conversion Lewis Rambo writes, "With the rise of new religious movements, the resurgence of 'born again' evangelical Christianity, the rapid spread of the charismatic movements and other forms of dramatic religious manifestation, there has been a renewed interest in conversion" (*Religious Studies Review* 8 [1982]: 145). This "renewed interest" underscores a fundamental fact of Christianity; it begins with an experience of "conversion." Jesus summoned his hearers to "repent and believe in the Gospel" (Mark 1:14–15), and within two generations the movement inaugurated by his life, death, and resurrection, in its spread eastward and westward, had gathered into its midst those who confessed that God made the crucified Jesus Lord and Messiah (Acts 2:36), as well as those "who turned to God from idols to serve a living and true God" (1 Thess. 1:9). Men and women turned from a familiar way of life and belief to the way proclaimed by Christian missionaries (Acts 9:2; 16:17). While the *fact* of conversion is an undisputed Christian legacy, the term itself has been differently understood, ranging in meaning from a change of religious belief and practice to a renewal of faith and devotion within a religious tradition.

In her treatment of the issue, Beverly Roberts Gaventa provides a much-needed examination of certain critical biblical texts which have been the source of Christian reflection on conversion and which in the current discussion are constantly used, and misused. After a survey of the language of "conversion" itself from the perspective of comparative religion and social psychology, Gaventa argues for a typology of conversion and questions whether the term "conversion," without further explanation, is adequate to those very New Testament texts that have been constantly invoked as a foundation for its use. Drawing on her earlier research on Paul's conversion, done under the direction of W. D. Davies and in dialogue with more recent studies such as that of J. Christiaan Beker (*Paul the Apostle: The Triumph of God in Life and Thought* [Philadelphia: Fortress Press, 1980]), she examines Paul's own statements in his letters and finds that the language of "transformation" more adequately describes Paul's experience.

Chapters 2 and 3 on the Acts of the Apostles contain Gaventa's most distinctive contributions to the present discussion in terms of method and content. She adopts a method of literary theological analysis, turning first to the three accounts of Paul's conversion in Acts 9, 22, and 26 and then to the conversion of other significant figures such as the Ethiopian eunuch and Cornelius. From careful study of the accounts of Paul's conversion Gaventa argues that they derive from a single source and represent Luke's adaptation of it to the literary context and theological thrust of a particular section of the narrative and of Acts as a whole. In chapter 3 she turns to other conversion accounts and again uncovers their literary and theological significance. Finally she turns to the language of conversion which has been so dominant in recent times, especially that of "born again," and locates this language in its historical and literary context. Thereby she indicates that this motif, though often misused, provides a rich source of reflection.

Gaventa's work shows that Acts is a model for the often quoted but seldom illustrated method of "narrative theology." The narratives themselves engage the reader in the theology of a given work. There are no shortcuts and readers who wish to find the "ideas" in Gaventa's work without walking through the text with her will miss a rich experience. She also extends an overture to those in Christian ethics who summon us to see biblical narrative as a mode of moral reflection. Her own conclusions about conversion in the New Testament are cogent and evocative—she questions whether it is appropriate to speak of the "conversion" of Paul and cautions that conversion in the New Testament is never a private affair. Her exegesis sets the perimeters for proper interpretation of the texts, nonetheless it does not exhaust their richness. This work offers a solid basis and a rich source of further reflection for a contemporary theology of conversion. It also invites readers to an eminently readable dialogue with some of the most engaging texts of the New Testament.

JOHN R. DONAHUE, S.J.

Preface

Within hours of presiding over the defense of my doctoral dissertation on the conversion of Paul as evidenced in his letters, Professor W. D. Davies suggested that I take up the phenomenon of conversion in Acts and elsewhere in the New Testament. What then began as an expansion of my dissertation has become a separate and distinct volume, in which the dissertation itself is represented in only part of one chapter. I am indebted to Professor Davies both for the suggestion and for his wise and skillful supervision of my earlier work.

Various portions of this book were presented at United Theological Seminary in Dayton, Ohio, as the J. Balmer Showers lectures, and at Berea College, Franklin College, and the University of Redlands. I thank the faculty, students, and guests who were present on those occasions for their interest and response. My students at Colgate Rochester Divinity School/Bexley Hall/Crozer Theological Seminary have also listened patiently as I tried out approaches taken in this volume. A number of them have read draft portions of the manuscript and their comments and questions shaped later revisions.

A significant amount of the research and writing of chapters 2 and 3 was completed during a year of sabbatical leave spent at the Yale Divinity School. Dean Leander Keck and John Bollier of the Yale Divinity School library welcomed and assisted me, and I remember that period with great fondness. Professors Richard Hays, David Lull, and Abraham Malherbe of Yale have read and commented on parts of the manuscript. Equally important were the conversations and seminars in which these three colleagues and others included me.

The year at Yale would have been impossible without the support of CRDS/BH/CTS and a grant from the Association of Theological

Schools. President Larry Greenfield has encouraged my work by making the time to read and comment carefully on the manuscript. Former Provost Leonard I. Sweet, now president of United Theological Seminary, knew when to exhort, when to comfort, and when to assist by reducing other responsibilities.

I am particularly indebted to Professor J. Louis Martyn of Union Theological Seminary, my teacher and colleague, who has listened as ideas for this volume were formed and reformed, and who read and commented on most of the manuscript. Professor Vernon Robbins of Emory University read chapter 2 and offered helpful suggestions. For assistance with this project and for collegiality in season and out, I am grateful to Professor Charles M. Nielsen of CRDS/BH/CTS and to Professor William Scott Green of the University of Rochester.

As editor of the Overtures series, Professor John R. Donahue, S.J., has encouraged my work at every step. Patient with delays and still zealous for the final product, he has operated with a large measure of graciousness. My editor at Fortress Press, John A. Hollar, contributed not only concerning matters of style but also with questions of substance.

Without the skill of Ms. Debra Watkins at the typewriter and word processor this volume would still be incomplete. She has been cheerful and tolerant, despite often adverse circumstances. My student assistant, Mr. Pieter Kiwiet, prepared the index and helped with proofreading.

Books are not made or nourished by scholars alone. I owe a great debt for the friendship of Susan Shafer, Susan King, James Gertmenian, Carol Sundquist, and Dorothy Martyn. Last in this list but first in my life are my husband, William Carter Gaventa, Jr., and my son, Matthew Roberts Gaventa.

Abbreviations

AnBib	Analecta biblica
BAGD	W. Bauer, W. F. Arndt, F. W. Gingrich, and F. W. Danker, *Greek-English Lexicon of the New Testament, and Other Early Christian Literature,* 2d ed. (Chicago: Univ. of Chicago Press, 1979)
BDF	F. Blass, A. Debrunner, and R. W. Funk, *A Greek Grammar of the New Testament* (Chicago: Univ. of Chicago Press, 1961)
BZ	*Biblische Zeitschrift*
BZNW	Beihefte zur Zeitschrift für die neutestamentliche Wissenschaft
CBQ	*Catholic Biblical Quarterly*
CNT	Commentaire du Nouveau Testament
FRLANT	Forschungen zur Religion und Literatur des Alten und Neuen Testaments
HNT	Handbuch zum Neuen Testament
HNTC	Harper's New Testament Commentaries
HTKNT	Herders theologischer Kommentar zum Neuen Testament
ICC	International Critical Commentary
IDBSup	Supplementary volume of the *Interpreter's Dictionary of the Bible*
JBL	*Journal of Biblical Literature*
MNTC	Moffatt New Testament Commentary
NCB	New Century Bible
NIGTC	New International Greek Testament Commentary
NTAbh	Neutestamentliche Abhandlungen

NTS	*New Testament Studies*
RSR	*Religious Studies Review*
SBLDS	Society of Biblical Literature Dissertation Series
SNTSMS	Society of New Testament Studies, Monograph Series
TDNT	G. Kittel and G. Friedrich, eds., *Theological Dictionary of the New Testament* (Grand Rapids: Wm. B. Eerdmans, 1964–76)
THKNT	Theologische Handkommentar zum Neuen Testament
TZ	*Theologische Zeitschrift*
WMANT	Wissenschaftliche Monographien zum Alten und Neuen Testament
ZNW	*Zeitschrift für die neutestamentliche Wissenschaft*

Introduction

FROM DARKNESS TO LIGHT

Language about conversion and transformation is commonplace in contemporary America. We have grown accustomed to those who talk about having "Damascus Road experiences." On the shelves of religious bookstores we find titles such as *Born Again, New Birth— New Life, How to Be Born Again,* and *How to Know You Are Born Again.* Alongside these new titles we may find now-standard works such as Thomas Merton's *Seven Storey Mountain,* Dorothy Day's *Long Loneliness,* and C. S. Lewis's *Surprised by Joy,* autobiographies that reveal something of the authors' movement toward conversion and the impact of conversion.

Nor is language about conversion confined to the realm of faith. *Time* magazine's article on the Titan missile explosion carried the title, "Light on the Road to Damascus," presumably because the editors took for granted that the reference would be intelligible to the readers of the magazine.[1] We hear and read about "born again" political liberals or conservatives and about "born again" economists. This particular phrase has become an abbreviated way of indicating merely that someone has changed his or her mind about something.

By contrast, "born again" language is virtually absent from the New Testament. As we shall see, writers of New Testament texts described conversion in a variety of ways, making generalizations about *the* meaning of conversion in the New Testament hazardous if not impossible. One common metaphor, present outside the New Testament as well as within it, is that conversion involves a change "from darkness to light." In Acts 26:18 Paul explains to Agrippa that his own mission was to preach to the Gentiles, that they might "turn from darkness to light." First Peter 2:9 recalls conversion as God's call "out of darkness into the marvelous light." Paul may have conversion in mind when he writes "For it is the God who said, 'Let light shine out of darkness,' who has shone in our hearts to give the light of the knowledge of the glory of God in the face of Christ" (2 Cor. 4:6). For all of these writers, conversion involves a movement so radical that only the image of darkness and light can capture it.

In this book we will explore those texts in the New Testament that gave rise to contemporary conversion language. We will also examine other major narratives about conversion and other images of transformation or conversion. The goal is to learn what conversion and transformation meant in the contexts of first-century Christianity and to compare that with understandings of being "born again."

Several decades ago, books dealing with conversion frequently began with the classic examples of Paul, Augustine, and Luther, and then turned to the lives of more recent converts. Occasionally, converts from Christianity to Judaism or vice versa were included. The assumption at work was that conversion belonged primarily to the Judeo-Christian tradition, and the main question addressed was the difference between "sudden" and "gradual" conversion.

Today, however, discussion regarding conversion and transformation has expanded, largely as a result of our highly pluralistic religious and cultural situation. For example, it was the growth of the evangelical movement that made "born again" an everyday expression. In evangelical circles, great stress is placed on the necessity of personal conversion. That stress has led some liberal Protestants, and even some within evangelical circles, to object that conversion was being personalized or privatized and to suspect that the corporate nature of Christian life was being neglected.[2] Others, viewing with alarm the declining membership rolls in mainline Protestant denominations, have attempted to imitate the "success" of evangelicals by initiating church growth and revitalization programs aimed at conversion. The nature and function of conversion is clearly at stake here.

In addition, the proliferation of cults and sects has brought to the fore a number of significant questions about conversion. A walk through one of our major airports is sufficient persuasion that conversion is a primary objective of such groups as the Unification Church, the Hare Krishna, and the Children of God. Concern about the recruitment tactics of the cults and controversy about deprogramming produce further interest in, and even alarm about, conversion and transformation.

At first glance, some will find it strange that biblical scholars have paid relatively little attention in recent years to conversion and transformation in the New Testament. After all, is it not in the New Testament that we find what is widely termed the "prototype" of Christian conversion—the conversion of Paul? Is it not John's Gospel that narrates the conversation between Jesus and Nicodemus in which Jesus says, "Unless one is born anew [*gennēthē anōthen;* KJV, "born again"], he cannot see the kingdom of God" (John 3:3)? Why, then, has not more work been done on this problem?[3]

Answers to such a question are conjectural at best, but there are two possibilities that bear considering. Both have to do with the fact that the questions raised in an inquiry about conversion are fundamental questions. In one sense, anyone who is acquainted with historical-critical exegesis is able to answer them. The author of the Fourth Gospel uses "born anew" *(gennēthē anōthen)* as one of several ways in which he distinguishes between those who belong to Jesus and those who belong to the world. The language of new birth occurs in the New Testament only in John and in 1 Peter. Similarly, while Luke narrates Paul's conversion three times, Paul himself never describes a Damascus Road experience or applies the terms "turning" *(epistrophē)* or "repentance" *(metanoia)* to himself. Hence, some might conclude that there is no problem to discuss once the material is read honestly.

There is, however, another way in which an inquiry about conversion is fundamental. To ask about conversion is to ask what attracts people to a faith, what changes in their understanding of themselves and of the world, and what supports them in the new faith. It is also to ask about a community of believers, its self-understanding, and its attitudes toward outsiders, seekers, and newcomers. Because questions such as these are often far beyond the reach of our sources and our tools, scholars may find other questions more immediately rewarding. While the present study cannot hope to resolve these matters, it can draw attention to an important and frequently neglected area.

CONVERSION AND
THE SOCIAL SCIENCES

Particularly because of the growth of the cults in this country, and their attraction for young people, sociologists, psychologists, and anthropologists have become fascinated with the dynamics of conversion and transformation. That is not to say that the problem only emerged in the 1970s, of course. William James's masterpiece, *The Varieties of Religious Experience,* still finds its way into the discussion, as do the earlier investigations of E. D. Starbuck and James Leuba.[4] James analyzed journals and other written accounts of conversion to Christianity and focused primarily on how conversion occurs and what its long-term results are.

Today, however, in keeping with the pluralistic religious scene noted above, the range of conversion-related research in the social sciences is itself impressive. Some anthropologists have addressed the problem of conversion to traditional religions in Third World countries, as well as conversion from those traditional religions to one of the "world" religions. Within this country, researchers have investigated the conversions of Protestant seminarians, Pentecostal Catholics, devotees of UFO cults, and members of various Jesus movements, to mention only a few. Indeed, conversion has become such a complex phenomenon among young people, in particular, that some social scientists have developed theories regarding "conversion careers"; that is, patterns certain groups are prone to follow in their conversions from movement to movement to movement.[5]

Despite the diversity of the groups studied, several questions appear over and over again. The first of these has to do with the category of "conversion" and phenomena pertaining to it. For example, discussion continues about whether gradual changes are conversions in the same way that sudden changes are.[6] In addition, questions are asked about whether conversion includes simple changes of affiliation, such as a Baptist who becomes a Methodist primarily as a result of marrying a Methodist, or whether conversion describes only radical changes of identity.[7]

A second question that occurs with some regularity concerns the psychological health of converts. The issue here is whether conversion is an abnormal development or a pattern leading to maturity.[8]

Although this question is not raised as frequently or as explicitly as was the case in an earlier period, it does still appear.

Two other clusters of questions appear, in some form, in virtually every study of conversion: who is converted and under what circumstances? Much attention has been paid to analyzing the age, the social class, and the previous experience of converts. Related to this is a concern to understand the conditions and circumstances under which conversion is most apt to occur.

A couple of concrete examples will help to illustrate this major area of recent work. As a result of their study of a millenarian cult on the West Coast, John Lofland and Rodney Stark constructed a model that would describe and account for conversion to such a perspective. Those conditions were as follows: A person must (1) be in a situation of "enduring, acutely felt tension"; (2) operate "within a religious problem-solving perspective" (i.e., to see religious dimensions in events); (3) consider himself or herself to be a "religious seeker"; (4) encounter the belief system at a turning point in his or her life; (5) form "an affective bond" with some adherents of the belief system; (6) be relatively free of extracult relationships; and (7) be subject to extensive interaction with other adherents.[9] The Lofland-Stark model has by no means won unanimous acceptance, but it has been the occasion for further research and discussion, much of which has focused on the applicability of this model to other types of conversion.[10]

Another group of social scientists has applied insights from the sociology of knowledge to the problem of conversion. This approach is reflected in the often-cited comment of Peter Berger and Thomas Luckmann: "To have a conversion experience is nothing much. The real thing is to be able to keep on taking it seriously; to retain a sense of its plausibility." Persons who quote only these two sentences may lead others to think that Berger and Luckmann were referring to an individual convert's need to maintain faith. However, what immediately follows indicates otherwise:

> *This* [retaining the plausibility of conversion] is where the religious community comes in. It provides the indispensable plausibility structure of the new reality. In other words, Saul may have become Paul in the aloneness of religious ecstasy, but he could *remain* Paul only in the

context of the Christian community. . . . This relationship of conversion and community is not a peculiarly Christian phenomenon.[11]

More specific application of the sociology of knowledge to conversion itself has come from Arthur Greil. Greil argues that individuals are likely to convert when they have acquired close friends or associates who have a different perspective and that the perspective of individuals is more likely to be discredited when those who aided in the maintenance of a perspective become unavailable. An individual's perspective is also likely to be discredited in times of rapid social change and in highly pluralistic social contexts.[12]

Even this rapid survey of recent research gives evidence of the bewildering variety of questions and hypotheses. In an article critical of both the nature of the questions being asked and the answers offered, Max Heirich noted that current theories offer three kinds of explanations for the phenomena of conversion:

1. Psychological stress. Many of the psychological studies of conversion describe it as a "fantasy solution" to stress. The stress itself may be the result of a personal situation or of social conditions.

2. Previous socialization. According to this approach, conversion has its origins in early conditioning. Thus, adherents examine religious orientations of parents, sex-role education (because of women's greater interest in religious matters), and education.

3. Direct social influence. This explanation stresses the social interactions that make it possible for persons to change religious perspective. Such analyses look at patterns of influence and their relationship to conversion.[13]

Obviously, these are not mutually exclusive options. The Lofland-Stark model, for example, uses elements of each of these options.[14] Nevertheless, they do reflect major tendencies in current research on conversion in the social sciences.

Although there are several ways in which this research can inform the present study, the greatest contribution may come from an awareness of some of the difficulties that have emerged in the social sciences. To put it another way, the *limitations* of that research may indicate some appropriate issues and some problem areas for an examination of conversion and transformation in the New Testament.

One persistent difficulty in the social scientific realm is the variety of conversion experiences. I do not refer now simply to the matter of definition, but to the problem created for analysis by the wide spectrum of religious groups and by the diverse experiences that are termed conversion. For example, to what extent can the Lofland-Stark theory, which was formulated on the basis of a small millenarian cult, be applied to conversions to Catholic pentecostalism?[15] Or how can one compare the experience of a member of a UFO cult with the experience of a Baptist who converts to Judaism? One clear need, then, is the development of a typology of conversion.[16]

Another limitation of current research, and more problematic because it is unavoidable, is the heavy reliance on autobiographical reports. The problems created by these statements should be obvious. As converts go about interpreting and explaining their new convictions, they necessarily re-create the past. Beliefs and events and motivations may be reinterpreted or forgotten in the attempt to put both past and present into a framework that is comprehensible from the point of view of the present. This is not to say, of course, that no reliable information comes from converts, but that the breach between past and present makes it impossible for converts to return to their preconversion state of mind.[17]

Brian Taylor argues that analysis of converts' statements must not confuse retrospection with introspection, that it must distinguish between *"what accounts of the past express and of what such accounts are themselves an expression."* What a convert says is not itself an explanation of conversion, but what a convert says is what analysis should attempt to explain.[18] This kind of observation necessitates a careful rethinking of the interview methods used by social scientists.

In addition to the problems of the great variety of conversion experiences and the nature of converts' autobiographical reflections, there is a third difficulty with recent research on conversion, a difficulty related to the kinds of questions being asked. As noted earlier, the predominant questions concern who is likely to convert (age, gender, social class) and under what conditions conversion is likely to occur. While these are not insignificant questions, they do not touch the *content* of conversion. Upon reading the literature, one has the impression that something is missing, that only some of the issues have been addressed. That is because social scientists have, by and large, asked about the process of conversion (Who converts and under what circumstances? What happens to an individual? How does change occur?) rather than its substance. This observation is not unrelated to Taylor's comments concerning the use of interviews with converts. The temptation is to analyze the materials as if they were objective data and to forget to ask what is really being said.

While this criticism is not frequently found, it does appear in the literature with some regularity and in several forms. Scroggs and Douglas describe the conceptual framework of current research as having a functional approach that tends to miss the point because it asks about process rather than about substance.[19] Along the same line, Heirich concludes that sociological analysis can only explain the route conversion takes among those who are already on a religious quest. However, the research being done explains neither what motivates the religious quest nor the response to it.[20] Heirich argues that the interesting questions are: (1) "What circumstances destroy clarity about root reality (both for individuals and for collectivities)?" and (2) "How is an alternative sense of grounding asserted in ways that lead various observers to take it seriously?"[21] Research has not yet arrived at the heart of the matter: What is involved when an individual gives up one view of self and the world for another?

The reason for discussing these problem areas is not to dismiss the labors of social scientists. Their study of conversion is complicated because of the nature of the phenomena being studied, and their findings are useful, if incomplete. It hardly needs to be said that models of conversion based on twentieth-century experience should not be read into the New Testament uncritically. Nevertheless, some of the issues with which social scientists are dealing, and some of the limitations they face, do have their counterparts in our examination of the New Testament.

THE DESIGN OF THE PRESENT STUDY

Bearing in mind the ubiquitous use of conversion language and the issues that emerged from our review of research on conversion in the social sciences, where do we begin our study and what questions do we ask?

Certainly the first task is to establish a working definition of conversion and to distinguish between conversion and other types of change. In part, I isolate that task because of the current situation, in which the term is applied to a great variety of experience. There is, however, another reason, which is that some biblical scholars have called into question the custom of speaking of the conversion of Paul, and have argued that the term is inappropriate or misleading.[22] While they may be quite right to protest the popular view of Paul's experience, the first issue raised is, again, what we mean by the term conversion.

James's definition of conversion has been widely used over the years and offers, therefore, a convenient starting point:

> To be converted, to be regenerated, to receive grace, to experience religion, to gain an assurance, are so many phrases which denote the process, gradual or sudden, by which a self hitherto divided, and consciously wrong inferior and unhappy, becomes unified and consciously right superior and happy, in consequence of its firmer hold upon religious realities.[23]

The emphasis James places on conversion as a change from division to wholeness, from a negative to a positive state, appears in a slightly different form in the well-known definition of Arthur Darby Nock:

> By conversion we mean the reorientation of the soul of an individual, the deliberate turning from indifference or from an earlier form of piety to another, a turning which implies a consciousness that a great change is involved, that the old was wrong and the new is right.[24]

These definitions differ in that James seems to imply that the convert's status is objectively improved, while Nock describes a change that is subjectively assessed. The distinction may reflect the disciplines of the two scholars, one of whom concentrates on the relationship of conversion to emotional health, while the other addresses the question of conversion in the history of religions. A more recent definition of conversion also characterizes it as a change from a rejected past to an accepted and affirmed present:

> Conversions are drastic changes in life. . . . Conversions are transitions to identities which are proscribed within the person's established universes of discourse, and which exist in universes of discourse that negate these formerly established ones. The ideal typical conversion can be thought of as the embracing of a negative identity. The person becomes something which was specifically prohibited.[25]

All three definitions characterize conversion as a pendulum-like change in which there is a rupture between past and present, with the past portrayed in strongly negative terms. This definition might appropriately be applied, then, to a young person who forsakes a comfortable Protestant church in the suburbs for the Unification Church, or to a Mormon who leaves family and friends for the Roman Catholic church.

Because it involves a negation of the past and a drastic change, this definition excludes many experiences that are frequently called conversions. For example, a Methodist who becomes a Presbyterian following a quarrel with the pastor of the local Methodist church would not be regarded as a convert. Nor does this definition apply to the change that Martin Luther experienced. Other categories are required to describe such circumstances.

Richard Travisano has offered one additional category: alternation. Unlike conversions, alternations are changes that do not involve a rejection of the past and, indeed, actually develop out of one's past. Travisano describes them as

> relatively easily accomplished changes of life which do not involve a radical change in universe of discourse and informing aspect, but which are a part of or grow out of existing programs of behavior. . . . To say such changes are easily accomplished, of course, does not mean that everyone makes them with no trouble whatsoever. Adjustments to college or to fatherhood, for example, are often quite painful or pervasive. But these changes and their attendant problems are provided for in established universes of discourse.[26]

Examples of alternations are almost endless: the Presbyterian who becomes a Methodist because he marries a Methodist, the Baptist who joins an Episcopal church because the neighbors favor it, the liberal Methodist who drifts into the theology of the Unitarian Church.

The distinction between a conversion and an alternation is helpful, but yet another category is needed. In addition to those experiences that grow out of the past (alternations), and those that result in an affirmed present at the expense of a rejected past (conversions), there are experiences that we may call transformations. A transformation is a radical change of perspective in which some newly gained cognition brings about a changed way of understanding. Unlike a conversion, a transformation does not require a rejection or negation of the past or of previously held values. Instead, a transformation involves a new perception, a re-cognition, of the past.

This notion of transformation is informed by Thomas Kuhn's concept of a paradigm shift. According to Kuhn's analysis of the history of science, a paradigm is a theoretical model that is operative for a period of time in a particular branch of science. The model not only provides working hypotheses about given phenomena, but determines the questions research will ask, the way in which data will be interpreted, and the methods used for further research. When problems arise with a given paradigm, the paradigm is not abandoned until a new and more compelling paradigm emerges. Even then the data generated by the earlier paradigm are not rejected; they are reappropriated as part of the new paradigm.[27]

The change in cognition involved in a transformation, or in a paradigm shift, can be illustrated by the diagrams used in Gestalt psychology. Whether one sees a rabbit or a duck in a diagram, for example, depends on one's own expectations. The process of seeing a figure first as a duck, reexamining it, finding a rabbit, and then reinterpreting the figure, is a process that alters one's understanding of the figure and its potential.[28] A transformation, similarly, involves a changed way of understanding and interpreting God and world.

Although it is hazardous to draw on a figure so variously interpreted, Martin Luther's life may provide a helpful example of what is intended by the term transformation. While studying Romans, he had become obsessed with the phrase, "the righteousness of God." Later on Luther wrote that he had grown to hate that phrase because he had been taught to regard it as the righteousness "with which God is righteous and punishes the unrighteous sinner":

> At last, by the mercy of God, meditating day and night, I gave heed to the context of the words. . . . There I began to understand that the righteousness of God is that by which the righteous lives a gift of God, namely by faith. And this is the meaning: the righteousness of God is revealed by the gospel, namely, the passive righteousness with which merciful God justifies us by faith, as it is written, "He who through faith is righteous shall live." Here I felt that I was altogether born again and had entered paradise itself through open gates. There a totally other face of the entire Scripture showed itself to me.[29]

Note the use of cognitive language here. Although Luther had earlier seen only the phrase, "the righteousness of God," he finally "gave heed to the context." He began to understand God's righteousness differently. As a result he saw another "face" of Scripture, previously unavailable to him. Although it may be argued that this transformation ultimately led to a negation of Luther's past, what he describes here is primarily a change in perception, a reinterpretation.

There are, then, *three categories of personal change* of which we need to be aware in this study: alternation, conversion, and transformation. Alternation is a relatively limited form of change that develops from one's previous behavior; conversion is a radical change in which past affiliations are rejected for some new commitment and identity; transformation is also radical change, but one in which an altered perception reinterprets both present and past. These distinctions are, of course, not hard and fast. Nevertheless, these categories may be useful as we begin our examination of the New Testament.

A rough parallel to this typology emerges from two important studies of conversion in early Christianity. In his classic volume, *Conversion*, Nock contrasts conversion with adhesion. As noted earlier, Nock defines conversion as a pendulum-like change in which there is "the reorientation of the soul," "a turning from indifference," "a consciousness . . . that the old was wrong and the new is right." Nock also argues that conversion occurred in the ancient world almost exclusively in Judaism and Christianity, and in the philosophical schools. In most religious traditions, or what Nock would call cultic traditions, there was *adhesion* rather than conversion. When individuals were attracted to new cults, they simply took up the practices of the new cults in addition to the practices of the cults in which they already participated. New cults did not displace old ones or, as Nock puts it, "new worships" were viewed as "useful supplements and not as substitutes."[30]

By contrast, Ramsay MacMullen reconstructs the rise of early Christianity with an emphasis on the many degrees of interest in and affiliation with Christianity. MacMullen criticizes Nock for having assumed that "religious belief does not deserve the name unless it is intense and consuming."[31]

The differences between these two volumes revolve around their use of the term conversion. While Nock limits conversion to what I have called pendulum-like conversion, MacMullen includes adhesion in his understanding of conversion. Thus, Nock sees conversion to Christianity only where there is a full and exclusive commitment to Christian faith, but MacMullen insists on including those who may have merely added certain Christian practices to their other acts of worship.

It is also important to see the parallel between Nock's category of adhesion and my category of alternation. If alternation is a change that grows out of established life patterns, so is adhesion. When the upwardly mobile young professional turns to the Episcopal church as an act of social mobility, he or she acts in keeping with an established life pattern, just as did the first-century Roman who decided it was only smart to begin to worship Isis along with the traditional deities.

What follows is not a corrective or supplement to Nock and Mac-Mullen, but a study of the major texts in the New Testament that are related to alternation, conversion, and transformation. In order to give the material adequate attention, only the major texts and problems are included: the experience of Paul, the narratives found in the Book of Acts, the language of new birth and new life that appears in John and 1 Peter. This approach has the advantage of dealing directly with the texts that are used—and frequently abused—in contemporary discussions of conversion.

With what questions do we begin? Here the issues that have emerged in the social sciences can be particularly instructive. Paul's remarks about himself must be understood to reflect his convictions at the time he was writing. Taylor's caution about the use of converts' statements is extremely important for our reading of Paul. What Paul himself says has much to tell us, but what it tells us concerns his *understanding* of what had occurred. It is, to borrow from Taylor, retrospection rather than introspection.

When we turn to the narratives of Acts, a similar problem occurs. Luke includes a number of conversion stories as part of his account of "the things which have been accomplished." What role do these stories play in the larger context of Acts? What do they indicate about Luke's understanding of conversion and transformation? How are these stories related to the situation in which Luke wrote?

The same questions will appear in our examinations of the so-called born-again motif in John and of conversion terminology elsewhere in the New Testament. At base, we are asking what various New Testament writers have to say about the changes that the gospel brings about and requires. Finally, we will compare those perspectives with contemporary discussions about conversion.

NOTES

1. *Time* (29 September 1980): 28.
2. See Richard Quebedeaux, *The Worldly Evangelicals* (San Francisco: Harper & Row, 1978), 17–18; and Jim Wallis, "Conversion: What Does It Mean to Be Saved?" *Sojourners* 7 (May 1978): 10–14.
3. One must be careful not to oversimplify the situation. In an earlier period, several large studies of conversion in the New Testament were written, although primarily for a general audience. Paul's conversion continues to receive considerable attention (see chap. 1). Nevertheless, this is not one of the burning issues in New Testament studies.
4. William James, *The Varieties of Religious Experience* (London: Longmans, Green & Co., 1902); E. D. Starbuck, *The Psychology of Religion,* 3d ed. (New York: Charles Scribner's Sons, 1912); James Leuba, "A Study in the Psychology of Religious Phenomena," *American Journal of Psychology* 5 (1896): 309–85.
5. James T. Richardson and Mary Stewart, "Conversion Process Models and the Jesus Movement," in *Conversion Careers: In and Out of the New Religions,* ed. James T. Richardson (Beverly Hills, Calif.: Sage Publications, 1978), 24–42. I have been greatly helped in this section by the bibliography compiled by Lewis Rambo, "Current Research on Religious Conversion," *RSR* 8 (1982): 146–59.
6. James R. Scroggs and William G. T. Douglas, "Issues in the Psychology of Religious Conversion," *Journal of Religion and Health* 6 (1967): 206–7; Geoffrey E. W. Scobie, *Psychology of Religion* (New York: John Wiley & Sons, 1975), 50–51.
7. Significant and provocative on this point is the article by Richard Travisano, "Alternation and Conversion as Qualitatively Different Transformations," in *Social Psychology Through Symbolic Interaction,* ed. Gregory P. Stone and Harvey A. Farberman (Waltham, Mass.: Ginn-Blaisdell, 1970), 594–606.
8. Scroggs and Douglas, "Issues in the Psychology of Religious Conversion," 207–8; Sigmund Freud, "A Religious Experience," in *Collected Papers,* ed. James Strachey (London: Hogarth Press, 1957), 5:243–46; L. Salzman, "The Psychology of Religious and Ideological Conversion," *Psychiatry* 16 (1953): 177–87; Joel Allison, "Recent Empirical Studies in Religious Conversion Experiences," *Pastoral Psychology* 17 (1966): 21–34; idem, "Religious Conversion: Regression and Progression in an Adolescent Experience," *Journal for the Scientific Study of Religion* 8 (1969): 23–38.

9. John Lofland and Rodney Stark, "Becoming a World-Saver: A Theory of Conversion to a Deviant Perspective," *American Sociological Review* 30 (1965): 862–74; John Lofland, *Doomsday Cult: A Study of Conversion, Proselytization, and Maintenance of Faith,* 2d ed. (New York: Irvington Publishers, 1977).

10. See Richardson, *Conversion Careers,* for a collection of essays illustrative of the research since Lofland and Stark.

11. Peter Berger and Thomas Luckmann, *The Social Construction of Reality: A Treatise in the Sociology of Knowledge* (Garden City, N.Y.: Doubleday & Co., 1966), 158.

12. Arthur Greil, "Previous Dispositions and Conversion to Perspectives of Social and Religious Movements," *Sociological Analysis* 38 (1977): 115–25.

13. Max Heirich, "Change of Heart: A Test of Some Widely Held Theories about Religious Conversion," *American Journal of Sociology* 83 (1977): 654.

14. Ibid., 654–55.

15. Lofland and Stark claimed only that their model was valid for a specific type of conversion, but others have attempted to use it as a general model. See Lofland, "Becoming a World-Saver," in Richardson, *Conversion Careers,* 21–22.

16. The work of Travisano, "Alternation and Conversion," moves into this area.

17. Berger and Luckmann, *Social Construction of Reality,* 159–60. Students of the genre of autobiography have made similar comments about the way in which it functions to interpret the past. See Roy Pascal, *Design and Truth in Autobiography* (Cambridge: Harvard Univ. Press, 1960), 19; K. H. Weintraub, *The Value of the Individual: Self and Circumstance in Autobiography* (Chicago: Univ. of Chicago Press, 1978), xvii–xviii.

18. Brian Taylor, "Recollection and Membership: Converts' Talk and the Ratiocination of Commonality," *Sociology* 12 (1978): 316–17. See also his "Conversion and Cognition: An Area for Empirical Study in the Micro-Sociology of Religious Knowledge," *Social Compass* 23 (1976): 5–22.

19. Scroggs and Douglas, "Issues in the Psychology of Religious Conversion," 214.

20. Heirich, "Change of Heart," 673.

21. Ibid., 673–74. I take this to be similar to Clifford Geertz's critique of contemporary work in anthropology of religion. Geertz describes the task of the anthropological study of religion as having two stages: the analysis of systems of meanings, and the relating of those systems to social and psychological processes. His concern is that current work in the field overlooks the first task "and in so doing takes for granted what most needs to be elucidated." See "Religion as a Cultural System," in Clifford Geertz, ed., *The Interpretation of Cultures* (New York: Basic Books, 1973), 125.

22. See, for example, Krister Stendahl, *Paul Among Jews and Gentiles* (Philadelphia: Fortress Press, 1976), 7–23. Note that Stendahl describes a conversion simply as a "change of 'religion' " (p. 7). On this whole problem, see chap. 1 below.

23. James, *Varieties of Religious Experience*, 189.

24. A. D. Nock, *Conversion: The Old and New in Religion from Alexander the Great to Augustine of Hippo* (London: Oxford Univ. Press, 1933), 7.

25. Travisano, "Alternation and Conversion," 600–601.

26. Ibid., 601.

27. Thomas Kuhn, *The Structure of Scientific Revolutions*, 2d ed. (Chicago: Univ. of Chicago Press, 1970).

28. For a useful development of this comparison, see Carl Raschke, "Revelation and Conversion: A Semantic Appraisal," *Anglican Theological Review* 60 (1978): 420–36.

29. "Preface to the Complete Edition of Luther's Latin Writings," in *Selected Writings of Martin Luther*, 4 vols., ed. Theodore G. Tappert (Philadelphia: Fortress Press, 1967), 1:26–27.

30. Nock, *Conversion*, 1–16.

31. Ramsay MacMullen, *Christianizing the Roman Empire (A.D. 100–400)* (New Haven, Conn.: Yale Univ. Press, 1984), 2–9.

CHAPTER 1

Conversion in
the Letters of Paul

INTRODUCTION

In one of her letters, Flannery O'Connor comments on the apostle Paul, "I reckon the Lord knew that the only way to make a Christian out of that one was to knock him off his horse."[1] Although the New Testament nowhere connects a horse with the change of Paul from zealous persecutor of the church to zealous apostle, O'Connor's remark is indicative of the widespread familiarity with and curiosity about that change. What is usually referred to as the "conversion" of Paul has been celebrated in the church year and portrayed in painting, literature, and drama. The apostle Paul might well be history's most famous convert.

Several problems accompany this popularization of Paul's life, two of which require special attention at the outset of our discussion. One problem concerns New Testament sources and how those are to be employed in any study of Paul. The other is whether the term "conversion" adequately describes the change in Paul.

Most of the popular understandings of the "conversion" of Paul come from the narratives of Acts 9, 22, and 26, where we find the familiar accounts of Paul's journey to Damascus and his confrontation along the way. By contrast, Paul's letters make only a few comments about the change he underwent. It would be difficult to derive a "conversion story" from them. But often these comments from Paul's letters are used merely to supplement the narratives of Acts.

This procedure has serious methodological problems and unfortunate consequences. To begin with, it employs two very different sources as if they were equivalent. However limited and situational Paul's comments about himself may be, they do provide us some access to his own understanding and perspective. The Acts of the Apostles most likely was written at least three decades later and, as we shall see in chapters 2 and 3, Luke constructed his narratives for his own very particular theological purposes. To use the story of Paul in Acts in preference to the letters is to ignore the character of Acts. Further, to weave Acts and the letters together is to overlook the distinctiveness of each source just as we do when we weave the four canonical gospels together in order to produce a "life" of Jesus.

A far better approach to the problem is to begin with the earliest source, *the letters of Paul.* This approach provides us not only with the earliest material but also helps us to understand what Paul himself says concerning his move from persecutor to apostle, and to discern what place those remarks occupy within the letters and what light they shed on the character of Paul's "conversion." Comparable questions can later be addressed to the narratives in Acts. The goal here is not to synthesize the two sources but to conduct separate inquiries that can eventually be compared with one another.[2]

This procedure also allows us to address the more difficult problem, or set of problems, surrounding the term "conversion" as applied to Paul. Many New Testament scholars insist that it is inappropriate to speak of Paul as having experienced a "conversion." Krister Stendahl, who has given this position considerable exposure, argues that a conversion is a "change of 'religion' " and that Paul did not change *religions*. Instead of a conversion, what Paul experienced was a "calling," an assignment to a new task.[3]

If conversion is to be understood exclusively as a change of religion, then certainly Stendahl is right. Paul did not change religions. What we call "Christianity" was in Paul's time a sect within Judaism, not a new religion. Paul writes about the revelation of Jesus as God's Messiah, not about a new religion. (By the same token, it could be argued that we need to reconsider our practice of referring to Paul and his generation as Christians, since "Christian" and "Christianity" imply the existence of a new religion.)

Two recent works on Paul, those of F. F. Bruce and J. Christiaan Beker, amply illustrate this debate and provide a useful introduction to our study of Paul's remarks in the letters. In *Paul: Apostle of the Heart Set Free*, Bruce assesses the significance of Paul's conversion on the first page of his introduction: Paul devoted himself "single-mindedly to fulfilling the commission entrusted to him on the Damascus Road." On the next page Bruce writes that the sources for the study of Paul include both his letters (the primary source) and the Book of Acts (a secondary work, but one of "high historical value" which "may be used with confidence").[4]

Bruce's discussion of Paul's conversion underscores this confidence in Luke's portrait of Paul. According to Bruce, Paul regarded as blasphemous the Christian proclamation that a crucified criminal was the Messiah. The claim that Jesus had been raised from the dead came either from deceivers or from persons who were themselves deceived. Paul viewed this sect as a threat to all that constituted Judaism. He responded by engaging in a persecution of repression, with the sanction of the Sanhedrin at Jerusalem. While traveling to Damascus in order to arrest fugitive Christians, Paul underwent a dramatic experience.

Bruce draws on both the accounts in Acts and Paul's letters to argue that the conversion was both an external and an internal event. It was an objective revelation of the risen Lord, but it was also a profoundly inward experience. There is no indication that Paul's conversion was prepared for in any way, and psychological explanations of it are "precarious." Included in this conversion were Paul's apostolic call and his commission to preach among the Gentiles. He began at once to preach to Gentiles a gospel free from the law. Although his doctrine of justification by faith was not fully developed at that time, it too was implicit in the conversion.[5]

This analysis of Paul's conversion has several elements in common with the popular view of the Damascus Road event, but the two are not interchangeable. Bruce does not psychologize the texts, as is often done, nor does he sentimentalize. He does draw very heavily on the stories in Acts. He also insists on the importance of Paul's conversion for his ministry, when he contends that Paul's proclamation of a gospel without the law stems from his conversion. This aspect of Bruce's analysis has been further developed in the work of his student, Seyoon Kim, who finds in Paul's conversion the source of his theology.[6]

Beker's recent work provides a dramatic counterpoint to the works of Bruce and Kim. In *Paul the Apostle: The Triumph of God in Life and Thought*, Beker argues that the central and "coherent theme of

Paul's gospel" is God's triumph, "the hope in the dawning victory of God and in the imminent redemption of the created order." Paul's hermeneutic translates this theme "into the contingent particularities of the human situation."[7]

In his discussion of Paul's conversion and call, Beker begins by noting correctly that we actually know very little about Paul and that Paul tells us very little about himself. He describes his own experience only when it is necessary. Paul is not self-preoccupied, self-reflective, introspective, or narcissistic. That is not to say that Paul is timid or beset with an exaggerated humility; indeed, he is utterly convinced of his own apostolic authority and is not reluctant to claim that authority when circumstance dictates.[8]

Beker argues that, instead of describing an introspective conversion experience, Paul describes the "extroverted character of his apostolic call." Beker goes on to say that

> Paul's conversion experience is absorbed by the greater reality of his apostolic calling. He does not celebrate his "conversion experience" to mark his own spiritual grandeur, because he understands it as the commission to proclaim the gospel, that is, to serve Christ among the Gentiles.[9]

This means, as Bruce would agree, that we cannot seek a psychological explanation for Paul's conversion. The texts themselves do not allow it because they are concerned only with Paul's apostolic task. It also means that we cannot look for the secret of Paul's theology in his conversion experience because he is not glorifying his conversion; nor is he simply retelling his experience. Beker concedes that thought cannot be divorced from experience, but insists that experience is "brought into thought as its dynamic power."[10]

This approach departs so strikingly from Bruce's that some clarification is in order. Beker apparently does not think it possible to reconstruct the circumstances of either Paul's persecution of Christians or his subsequent conversion. He points to the sparseness of Paul's comments about himself and to the character of the comments he does make as evidence that Paul was concerned only with his call to preach the gospel. In addition, Beker denies the possibility of finding a psychological cause for Paul's conversion and locating the core of Paul's later theology in his conversion experience.

How shall we assess these two very different arguments? Beker carefully discriminates between the material in Acts and that in the letters. He also takes into account the nature of Paul's comments, which are neither introspective nor self-preoccupied. Nevertheless, Paul does say something about a change and, if we are willing to attend to those remarks, we may learn how Paul *understood* that change and how it functions in his letters. One suspects that Beker and others have avoided that task because of their dissatisfaction with earlier interpretations.

Bruce's treatment of Paul, by contrast, does take serious interest in his movement from persecutor to apostle. Bruce does ask about the possible connections between experience and thought. He does not, however, deal adequately with the difference between Acts and the letters. Indeed, Bruce relies heavily on the accounts in Acts and simply inserts Paul's words as they seem relevant. Bruce also does not address the issue of the function of Paul's comments in the letters themselves.

Many other scholars could be introduced into this discussion, but these two provide sufficient illustration of the problems involved in this study. While some reject the issue of conversion, others see in it the key to Paul's theology. In our examination of the relevant passages, we will attempt, with Bruce, to take the issue of Paul's change seriously while respecting, with Beker, the character and limits of our sources. Among the most important questions are these: (1) What does Paul actually say about his movement into the Christian community? (2) In what contexts do his remarks occur and how do they function? (3) What do the remarks suggest about the way Paul has interpreted the change he underwent? Following this examination, we can return to the question of the appropriateness of the term "conversion."

WHAT DOES PAUL SAY?

A young intellectual named Saul was on a journey along the road to Damascus, persecuting Christians, when he met Jesus Christ. To this day we speak about "Damascus Road experiences," because Paul was never the same again. He became the great Apostle Paul. *Many times* he referred to that encounter, even recalling the very day and moment when he met Christ [italics mine].[11]

This comment from Billy Graham notwithstanding, Paul's letters contain only a few references to his movement from persecutor to apostle. Most extensive and explicit among these are Gal. 1:11–17 and Phil. 3:2–11. We also need to consider Romans 7, which is frequently understood to refer to Paul's early "problem" with the law.[12]

Galatians 1:11–17

> For I would have you know, brethren, that the gospel which was preached by me is not man's gospel. For I did not receive it from man, nor was I taught it, but it came through a revelation of Jesus Christ. For you have heard of my former life in Judaism, how I persecuted the church of God violently and tried to destroy it; and I advanced in Judaism beyond many of my own age among my people, so extremely zealous was I for the traditions of my fathers. But when he who had set me apart before I was born, and had called me through his grace, was pleased to reveal his Son to me, in order that I might preach him among the Gentiles, I did not confer with flesh and blood, nor did I go up to Jerusalem to those who were apostles before me, but I went away to Arabia; and again I returned to Damascus.

Three questions are crucial to our reading of this text: (1) What does Paul mean by "revelation" *(apokalypsis)*? (2) What role does the review of vv. 13–14 play in the text? (3) How is the prophetic imagery of vv. 15–17 connected with Paul's self-understanding?

Paul opens this section of the letter with the emphatic claim that he received his gospel by means of revelation:

> For I would have you know, brethren, that the gospel which was preached by me is not man's gospel. For I did not receive it from man, nor was I taught it, but it came through a revelation of Jesus Christ. (vv. 11–12)

The very first words, "For I would have you know" *(gnōrizō de hymin)*, signal that a statement of importance follows. Paul uses a similar construction in 1 Cor. 12:3, where he introduces the problem of ecstatic speech, and in 1 Cor. 15:1, where he introduces the topic of resurrection traditions.[13]

Here the issue is the gospel Paul preached and how he received that gospel. Paul's gospel is "not man's gospel." Or, more literally, it is not "according to a human being" *(kata anthrōpon)*. This expression appears elsewhere in Paul's letters (Rom. 3:5; 1 Cor. 3:3; 9:8; 15:32a) in contexts where it appears to be the equivalent of "according to flesh" (*kata sarka*; e.g., Rom. 8:4–5, 12–13; 1 Cor. 1:26; 2 Cor. 1:17; 10:2). Neither *kata anthrōpon* nor *kata sarka* refers simply to human relations or human logic, but each expression involves some contrast between the deeds and standards of those who are confined to the sphere of the merely human and those deeds and standards that belong to the new life available in Christ.[14]

Paul claims that his gospel is not "human" because it did not come from human beings ("I did not receive it from man, nor was I taught it"). Instead, Paul received his gospel "through revelation." Before we conclude that "revelation" refers to a specific vision or dream, a miraculous encounter such as that described in Acts 9, we need to recall that the indefinite article *a* does not exist in Greek. It is, therefore, not at all clear that Paul is recalling some particular revelatory *event* or *occurrence*.

Paul's use of *apokalypsis* (apocalypse, revelation) and the related verb *apokalyptein* (to reveal) elsewhere makes it even less certain that he has reference here to a vision or miraculous encounter. *Apokalypsis* and *apokalyptein* in Paul's letters most often refer to the eschaton. Revelation is linked directly to God's action in the end time (e.g., Rom. 2:5; 8:18, 19; 16:25; 1 Cor. 1:7; 3:13; Gal. 3:23). Paul's reference in Gal. 1:11–12 must be read in the context of this larger revelatory event. He writes here not about a private event but about God's revelation and the attack of that revelation upon Paul's prior life.

Paul specifies that the revelation was "of Jesus Christ" (*Iesou Christou*), which may mean either that it came from Jesus Christ (subjective genitive) or that it was about Jesus Christ (objective genitive). A good example of this ambiguity is the English phrase "the persecution of Paul," which may refer either to Paul's persecution of believers (subjective genitive) or to the persecution Paul himself later experienced (objective genitive). Because v. 16 specifies that God revealed "the Son" to Paul, most commentators conclude that "of Jesus Christ" in v. 12 is an objective genitive.

Paul's stress here on revelation seems to conflict with other places in his letters where he draws on tradition. For example, in 1 Cor. 15:1–11 he insists on the authority of the tradition about the resurrection of Jesus (cf. also 1 Cor. 11:2, 23; 1 Thess. 2:13). Some have attempted to resolve this conflict by arguing that Paul understands all tradition to have its origin in the risen Lord. According to this view, when Paul writes in 1 Cor. 11:23 that he received the tradition about the supper "from the Lord," he means that the risen Lord is the immediate origin of the tradition. Thus, tradition is a byproduct of revelation.[15] However, this resolution of the problem does not adequately address the very different settings in which Paul refers to tradition and to revelation. In Galatians 1, he explains how he received the gospel; in 1 Corinthians 11 and especially in 15 he has reason to call to mind the shared form that gospel took in the community. That is, tradition and revelation have different functions. What is at stake in Gal. 1:11–17 is not the precise content of Paul's proclamation but its source.[16]

At this point, if we were hearing the letter read aloud for the first time, we might expect to hear some description or explanation of what Paul calls "revelation of Jesus Christ." Paul's insistence on revelation could preface an account or explanation of that revelation. Instead of offering an explanation Paul turns to his "former life in Judaism." Paul never says why he introduces his previous behavior or how it is related to revelation in vv. 11–12. Indeed, the argument that Paul relied on revelation might be stronger if vv. 13–14 were omitted. Therefore, an important question emerges: Why does Paul include this characterization of his "former life," and what place does it have in his argument?

The material contained in Gal. 1:13–14 is apparently not new to the recipients of the letter. "You have heard" indicates that they had earlier received some kind of information about Paul, although he does not specify what they have heard or from whom. The supposition that the Galatians received some report about Paul would find support in those places in his letters where he refers to the circulation of reports about the origin and growth of Christian communities (e.g., 1 Thess. 1:6–10).[17]

What circulated concerning Paul had to do with his "former life in Judaism" or, more literally, his "life style then in Judaism." The Greek word *anastrophē* (life or way of life) appears nowhere else in the genuine letters of Paul.[18] Significantly, it does occur in Tob. 4:14 and 2 Macc. 6:23, both texts in which the proper Jewish way of life is being urged at a time when that way of life has been severely threatened. Similarly, the term *Ioudaismos* (Judaism) is also associated with Jewish loyalty during persecution. Although we are accustomed to the term and take its meaning for granted, the Greek word *Ioudaismos* is extremely rare in the Hellenistic period.[19] We do find it in 2 Macc. 2:21; 8:1; 14:38, and 4 Macc. 4:26, where in each case it pertains to faithfulness in resistance to Hellenizing pressures. In all these texts, Martin Hengel's definition of *Ioudaismos* holds: "The word means both political and genetic association with the Jewish nation and exclusive belief in the one God of Israel, together with observance of the Torah given by him."[20]

Why does Paul use these words, particularly the rare *Ioudaismos*? Some argue that he has already separated Christianity from Judaism and conclude that his disdain for Judaism is reflected here.[21] But that argument falters when we look elsewhere in this and other letters. One important point of Galatians 3—4 is that those who are "in Christ" *are* the heirs of Abraham. In addition, Paul's lengthy treatment of Israel in Romans 9—11 reveals the struggle of one who understands himself to be located firmly within Israel. Those passages make it certain that Paul has not severed Christianity from Israel. Something else is at work here, as will become apparent when we examine Paul's description of his "way of life in Judaism."

Paul characterizes his way of life first as that of a persecutor of the church: "I persecuted the church of God violently and tried to destroy it" (Gal. 1:13). This translation from the RSV implies that Paul took violent physical action against the church, and that understanding finds support in the narratives of Acts. It is not at all clear, however, that Paul's "persecution" was in fact a physical one.

To begin with, the Greek expression *kath' hyperbolēn*, which the RSV renders "violently," means "to an extraordinary degree," "to excess," "to a great extent."[22] In other words, *kath' hyperbolēn* intensifies Paul's statement, but it in no way limits it to or defines it as a physical persecution. The verbs *diōkein* (pursue or persecute) and *porthein* (destroy) may refer to physical violence, although neither requires such a meaning.[23] What this language tells us is that, at the time of writing, Paul *viewed* his earlier action as excessive. It does not tell us that his action was, in fact, one of physical violence.

Paul's use of hyperbole elsewhere should make us cautious in our reading of this text. When he asks the Corinthians whether he should come to them with a rod (1 Cor. 4:21), we do not imagine that he planned to flog them. A similar observation surely pertains to the wish he expresses in Gal. 5:12. The difference between Gal. 1:13 and those texts is that the narratives of Acts have influenced our reading and have predisposed us to expect physical violence, even though it is extremely difficult to explain how Paul could have legally carried out a violent persecution.[24]

Paul's persecution of the church remains shrouded in unclarity. While it seems probable that his persecution was verbal rather than violent, we do not have sources that allow for certainty on that question. We also want to learn what Paul's motivation was, but this question is best postponed until the conclusion of the chapter.

Paul's "way of life in Judaism" also consisted of his advancement in Judaism by virtue of his excessive zeal for tradition. Central to this statement is the word *zēlotēs* (zealous), which frequently appears in the Jewish literature of the Hellenistic period in connection with zeal for the law of God, which may require suffering, and zeal that results in punishment of those who disobey the law.[25] Moreover, *zēlotēs* as zeal for the law and against the disobedient is prominent in 1 and 2 Maccabees in contexts similar to those in which *anastrophē* and *Ioudaismos* appear (e.g., 1 Macc. 2:23–28, 49–50; 2 Macc. 4:1–2). Thus, Paul's use of *zēlotēs* connects him with the zealous Jews of the Maccabean period. He saw himself as following in the tradition of those who acted forcefully to defend that which was proper to Judaism.

When we pull together what we have learned in Gal. 1:13–14, we see that Paul has portrayed himself as one who maintained faithfully all that pertained to Judaism. He may even have understood himself to be an heir of the Maccabean revolt. As proof of this claim of faithfulness, he offers his persecution of the church and his exceptional zeal. Paul presents himself as one whose life had been content and successful, when measured by inherited standards. He had followed a particular path, confident that it was the right path.

At the beginning of Gal. 1:15, another disjuncture appears. As he had shifted from *apokalypsis* to *anastrophē* in v. 13, now he shifts from *anastrophē* back to *apokalypsis*. After discussion of this *apokalypsis* and its consequences, we can return to these disruptions and their function in the text.

If we expect to find in Gal. 1:15–17 a description of a revelatory *event*, we are greatly disappointed. What we find instead concerns the action of God and Paul's response. All of the descriptions of God's actions in these verses explicitly or implicitly refer to the fact that Paul now has a task. Paul's assertion that he had been set apart before birth (literally, from my mother's womb) echoes the calls of Isa. 49:1 and Jer. 1:5.[26] Like the prophets, his vocation had been determined even before his birth. Paul also refers to God as the one who called *(kalein)* him through grace *(charis)*. While Paul understands that all of God's action for human salvation occurs by means of grace (e.g., Rom. 3:24; 4:16; 5:2; 5:15), he often associates grace with his own apostolic mission (e.g., 1 Cor. 3:10; 15:10; Gal. 2:9). Further, God also "revealed his Son." We have already seen that the language of *apokalypsis* and *apokalyptein* has much significance for Paul. Here it is important to notice additionally that when *apokalyptein* is used of God in the Septuagint, it frequently refers to God's self-revelation *and commissioning.*[27]

Paul writes that God revealed the Son *en emoi,* which may be translated in at least the following ways: (1) "within me," (2) "through me," or (3) "to me." Each of these translations is grammatically possible, and each has parallels elsewhere in the Pauline letters. Deciding among them becomes more difficult because of the claims attached to each. For example, some who argue for "within me" see this phrase as proof that Paul refers to a purely internal, subjective experience. Others insist that the proper translation is "to me" and that an external, objective appearance of the risen Lord is implied. "Through me" allows the possibility that Paul has in mind only his work and the way in which he has become a revelation for others.[28]

Probably the most useful clue for untangling these options occurs in the context. Verse 16b plainly identifies the purpose of this revelation, which is that Paul should proclaim the gospel. It would seem, therefore, that *en emoi* refers to the revelation to Paul (simple dative) that enabled him to preach to the Gentiles.[29] This view is reinforced by the parallel between *en emoi* (to me) and *en tois ethnesin* (to the Gentiles);[30] God revealed the Son *to Paul* in order that Paul might proclaim the Son *to the Gentiles.*

In Gal. 1:15–16a Paul insists that his gospel came from God ("he was pleased," "he set apart," "he called," "he revealed"). Verses 16b–17 turn the claim around as Paul insists that the gospel did not come from human beings. He immediately responded to the revelation, but not by consulting with others or by going to Jerusalem. Instead, Paul writes, "I went away into Arabia; and again I returned to Damascus."

We are now able to return to the questions with which we began: (1) What does Paul mean by "revelation"? (2) What role do vv. 13–14 play here? and (3) How is the prophetic imagery of vv. 15–17 connected with Paul's self-understanding?

When Paul asserts that his gospel came "through revelation," he is of course referring to his reception of the gospel, and yet he gives no explanation of that revelation. We cannot say even whether some specific occasion is intended or whether Paul only gradually recognized the "revelation of Jesus Christ." It is, however, important that we see this revelation as connected with the total eschatological inbreaking.

Verses 13–14 set the stage for this inbreaking by characterizing Paul's life "in Judaism." He had been acceptable, even successful, by the standards of his own people. Especially his actions as a persecutor confirmed his zeal. Paul does not describe this period as a time when he was separated from God, but as a time of apparent faithfulness.

That particular faithfulness is interrupted and, indeed, overthrown by the revelation of Jesus Christ. Paul draws on prophetic imagery in vv. 15–17 in order to convey the radical impact of the revelation. While this may imply that he views himself as standing within the prophetic tradition, it does not mean that what has occurred to Paul may be subsumed under the category of "call." What Paul describes in Gal. 1:11–17 includes a commission but it is not limited to that commission.

At least the following observations regarding Paul's "conversion" can be carried into the remainder of the chapter: (1) Paul gives no indication of remorse or guilt concerning his past; (2) he characterizes the "revelation of Jesus Christ" as a radical disruption of his previous life; his previous *cosmos* has been crucified (cf. Gal. 6:14); (3) the gospel of Jesus Christ is directly connected with Paul's mission among the Gentiles; (4) there is in v. 17 some vague and unspecific connection between the revelation and the area around Damascus.

Philippians 3:2–11

> Look out for the dogs, look out for the evil-workers, look out for those who mutilate the flesh. For we are the true circumcision, who worship God in spirit, and glory in Christ Jesus, and put no confidence in the flesh. Though I myself have reason for confidence in the flesh also. If any other man thinks he has reason for confidence in the flesh, I have more: circumcised on the eighth day, of the people of Israel, of the tribe of Benjamin, a Hebrew born of Hebrews; as to the law a Pharisee, as to zeal a persecutor of the church, as to righteousness under the law blameless. But whatever gain I had, I counted as loss for the sake of Christ. Indeed I count everything as loss because of the surpassing worth of knowing Christ Jesus my Lord. For his sake I have suffered the loss of all things, and count them as refuse, in order that I may gain Christ and be found in him, not having a righteousness of my own, based on law, but that which is through faith in Christ, the righteousness from God that depends on faith; that I may know him and the power of his resurrection, and may share his sufferings, becoming like him in his death, that if possible I may attain the resurrection from the dead.

In the middle of his letter to believers at Philippi[31] Paul lashes out at certain persons who, in his view, threaten to undermine the work he has done: "Look out for the dogs, look out for the evil-workers, look out for those who mutilate the flesh." Apparently the label "dogs" refers to Jewish Christians who proclaim that Gentiles must observe the law. In particular, they claim that Gentile males must be circumcised and that circumcision will open the door to spiritual perfection.[32]

If Paul's response to this group in Phil. 3:2–11 provides us with adequate clues to their claims, it appears that they have boasted of their own close connections with Israel. We can well imagine that they have also cast doubt on Paul's loyalty to Israel, his proclamation of a gospel apart from the law being offered as prime evidence. What we find in Phil. 3:2–11 is Paul's rebuttal. "If any other man thinks he has reason for confidence in the flesh, I have more. . . ." Paul gives his credentials in order to combat what is said against him. In so doing, he makes comments that reveal something of his understanding of his earlier move from persecutor to apostle.

"Circumcised on the eighth day" stands at the head of the list of Paul's credentials "in the flesh," just as "we are the true circumcision" began the description of Christian behavior (v. 3). Paul's assertion that he was circumcised on the eighth day is a claim that he conformed to one of the most basic requirements, if not the most basic requirement, of the covenant of Israel (see Gen. 17:9–12a; 21:4; Lev. 12:3). Paul's possible grounds for boasting, then, include not merely the fact that he was circumcised, but that he was circumcised at the time specified by the law.

The credentials that follow this first assertion are divided into two groups, each of which moves from inclusive to exclusive characteristics. The first group ("of the people of Israel, of the tribe of Benjamin, a Hebrew born of Hebrews") contains credentials that Paul has by virtue of his birth. In the second ("as to the law a Pharisee, as to zeal a persecutor of the church, as to righteousness under the law blameless") are those credentials achieved by Paul.

At the beginning of the first group stands the broad category, "of the people of Israel." Paul refers to more with this expression than an accident of birth. Israel signifies, for him, both the people born to Abraham and to his descendants (Rom. 9:6b, 27), and the role of Israel as the people chosen by God to be God's elect (Rom. 9:4, 6b).[33] The second phrase, "the tribe of Benjamin," specifies the group to which Paul belonged within Israel (cf. Rom. 11:1). Some have suggested that Paul took pride in being from the tribe of Benjamin because of its connection with Saul and the later loyalty of the tribe to the house of David.[34] At this point, however, Paul is simply listing his distinctions within Israel.[35]

Among these distinctions, Paul could also boast of being "a Hebrew born of Hebrews." It is likely that this expression refers to Paul's ability to use a Semitic language, probably Aramaic.[36] Such an interpretation is consistent with the limited New Testament usage of *hebraiois* and with the usage of both Philo and Josephus.[37] Of course, the knowledge of a language implies more than the ability simply to exchange a sentence in one language for a sentence in another language. There is, in addition, the knowledge of how a given group of people think and feel about the world, a cultural awareness in the strict sense. Paul's expression, "a Hebrew born of Hebrews," then means that he can claim to be an "insider" among his own people.

With this phrase, Paul completes his first set of credentials, those with which he was born. Having identified himself as a circumcised person, he began with the broadest category, membership in Israel. Then he noted the specific tribe to which he belonged within Israel and the name of that tribe. Finally, he narrowed the qualifications to those who could speak Aramaic.

Paul shifts at the end of Phil. 3:5 to credentials demonstrating that he is a good Jew not only by virtue of his birth, but also by virtue of his own choices within Judaism. Here he states his former disposition toward three ways of classifying oneself: according to law, according to zeal, and according to righteousness. Once again the groups named narrow successively so that he begins with the largest, the Pharisees, and proceeds to a smaller one, the persecutors, and finally to those who are "blameless."

According to the law, Paul is a Pharisee. The term *Pharisaios* appears in Paul's letters only here, although it is used of him in Acts 23:6 and 26:5. To call oneself a Pharisee with regard to the law meant primarily that one had chosen a particular stance concerning ritual purity—namely, that all Jews should live as if they were priests.[38] Paul thus had chosen this approach to the law in preference to other approaches, such as that of the Sadducees or of the community at Qumran.

According to zeal, Paul was a persecutor of the church. Our study of Gal. 1:11–17 has already demonstrated that "zeal" is associated with strong forceful action taken to preserve the traditions of Judaism. In Paul's case, that zeal led him to persecute the church. Some commentators argue that Paul's persecution of the church necessarily followed from his Pharisaism, but the text does not require that reading.[39] There could well be non-Pharisees who would exercise zeal in the same form or Pharisees who would elect another way of showing zeal. Thus, Paul's activity placed him within a group smaller than that composed of Pharisees.

The final example in Paul's list of credentials is "according to righteousness under the law blameless." Commentators are sometimes eager to point out that Paul's blamelessness existed "only by the criterion of the past" or "only according to human standards" or "only from a Pharisaic standpoint."[40] Verse 7 makes it clear that Paul no longer operates with the same criteria, but that does not mean that he views his past with guilt and remorse. What he says in v. 6b is not that he was *teleios* (perfect) but *amemptos*, which is best translated "without reproach" (cf. Phil. 2:14–15a; 1 Thess. 2:10; 3:13; 5:23).

We should take this comment at face value: Paul was, by the law's standard of righteousness, acceptable and without reproach. This is the zenith of his list of credentials. He was a good and loyal Jew, not only because he had been born into a Jewish family and protected its heritage, but also because he had selected the most rigorous position regarding the law, a strident position concerning zeal, and a blameless position with regard to righteousness.

In Phil. 3:7, Paul turns abruptly from the listing of his credentials to his loss of those same credentials. The force with which this rejection is stated implies that his opponents are mistaken when they debate with him on the basis of such data. He has been deprived of his credentials (v.7). Throughout vv. 7–8 there runs the notion of values and commitments. Paul's understanding of what is of value, what calls for commitment, has been changed. The phrase "whatever gain I had" summarizes succinctly all of vv. 4–6. These were the things Paul had considered to be "gain." Now, they become the opposite, "loss," or even *skybalon*.[41] Paul describes this radical change with the simple expression: "I counted [these things] as loss for the sake of Christ."

Verses 9–11 turn to that which Paul does regard as having value. This is summarized with the last clause of v. 8, "that I may gain Christ," and then explained in the long and convoluted phrases of vv. 9–11. The phrase "that I may know him" at the beginning of v. 10 is a purpose clause, which grammatically parallels "that I may gain Christ" and "[that I may] be found in him." Since these three purpose clauses also are parallel in meaning, the phrases that modify them will help us to clarify Paul's position in this transitional section.

Paul first identifies his goal as being to gain Christ and to be found "in him." Immediately following, he adds, "Not having a righteousness of my own based on law, but that which is through faith in Christ, the righteousness from God that depends on faith." It seems clear that the righteous life described in vv. 5–6 *belonged* to Paul; it was his by virtue of both birth and accomplishment. It was also a righteousness that had its origin in the law. Paul has rejected that righteousness in favor of one that comes through faith in Christ.

In v. 10 we find the third purpose clause, "that I may know him." The "knowing him" is specified as the power of his resurrection, sharing the sufferings, becoming like Jesus in his death, attaining the resurrection of the dead. The progression of aspects of "knowing him" is interesting here. Paul begins with the resurrection, and then includes two references to sharing the passion and death of Christ before again referring to the resurrection, this time in a somewhat tentative way *(ei pōs)*. Because we have seen nowhere in this text a reference to the resurrection, it may be that Paul recognized the danger of opening the way for enthusiasm by his reference to knowing the power of Christ's resurrection. That is, some would have seen any reference to the resurrection as an indication that believers have already been raised from the dead and have already achieved new life. To prevent this false conclusion, Paul quickly evokes the suffering of Christ and the necessity of believers to conform to that suffering.[42]

When we pull together what we have learned here, we see that Paul's primary intent is not to write about himself nor is it to criticize Judaism. Instead, he is engaged in a debate with Jewish Christians who are offering perfection through the law to Gentile Christians. Paul believes that his opponents adequately understand neither the suffering and humility of Jesus nor the implications of that suffering and humility for their own lives. He thus makes use of the Christ-hymn in 2:5–11 and of his own life in 3:2–11 to present the Philippians with models sufficient for their needs (3:17).[43]

The following aspects of the text are important for our discussion of Paul's "conversion": (1) Paul no longer regards his past achievements as significant, but neither does he appear to have regret or guilt because of his past; (2) Paul characterizes this change in his life as a matter of a change in his perception—a cognitive shift; (3) the only indication given as to the cause of this cognitive change is in the title, Christ, which leads us to conclude that whatever experience stands behind this, it is thoroughly messianic. Nothing in this text tells us about the circumstances of this change. To attempt to reconstruct such would be fruitless. We can conclude merely that behind the statement "I count everything as loss" stands something that produced a powerful cognitive shift.

Romans 7:13–25

> Did that which is good, then, bring death to me? By no means! It was
> sin, working death in me through what is good, in order that sin might be

shown to be sin, and through the commandment might become sinful beyond measure. We know that the law is spiritual; but I am carnal, sold under sin. I do not understand my own actions. For I do not do what I want, but I do the very thing I hate. Now if I do what I do not want, I agree that the law is good. So then it is no longer I that do it, but sin which dwells within me. For I know that nothing good dwells within me, that is, in my flesh. I can will what is right, but I cannot do it. For I do not do the good I want, but the evil I do not want is what I do. Now if I do what I do not want, it is no longer I that do it, but sin which dwells within me. So I find it to be a law that when I want to do right, evil lies close at hand. For I delight in the law of God, in my inmost self, but I see in my members another law at war with the law of my mind and making me captive to the law of sin which dwells in my members. Wretched man that I am! Who will deliver me from this body of death? Thanks be to God through Jesus Christ our Lord! So then, I of myself serve the law of God with my mind, but with my flesh I serve the law of sin.

"I do not understand my own actions. For I do not do what I want, but I do the very thing I hate." At least for Western readers, these lines compel attention.[44] We see and hear ourselves within them. For that reason and others, Romans 7 is one of the best-known passages in Paul's letters. With only a little imagination, Romans 7 can be read as Paul's recollection of the inner turmoil that preceded his conversion. Tortured by his inability to maintain the law, he sought to reduce his anxiety by persecuting Christians, but was eventually freed by an encounter with Jesus Christ.

Those who have taken this view for granted will find it odd that contemporary New Testament scholars almost universally reject the notion that Paul describes his own conversion here. Although there is unending debate about the identity of the *egō* (I) in Romans 7, there is near consensus at this one point: Romans 7 does not provide information about the conversion of Paul.[45]

Because this near consensus runs counter to the more popular reading of the text, some explanation is needed. We will first look at the argument for understanding Romans 7 as connected with Paul's conversion and then at the problems with that argument.

The connection between Romans 7 and Paul's conversion goes back at least to Origen and has been supported by John Wesley, Johannes Weiss, James Moffatt, and others.[46] In recent decades the best-known proponent of this conviction is C. H. Dodd. Against the argument that the *egō* of Romans 7 refers to everyone, similar to the English "one," Dodd insisted that Paul was referring to himself. Paul saw his own experience in the story of the Fall (Rom. 7:7–12). While Dodd conceded that Paul sometimes uses the first person singular in a generalized way (cf. 1 Cor. 8:13; 13:1–3; 14:6–9), he also argued that Paul always includes himself. Further, Dodd drew attention to Rom. 7:24 as evidence of a personal confession.[47]

According to Dodd, not only does the *egō* here include Paul, a point with which many would agree, but Paul refers to "his condition before his conversion, culminating at the moment at which he was 'apprehended by Christ Jesus.' " Although the present tense of the verbs in vv. 14–25 suggests a present condition, Dodd argues that the context requires the conclusion that Paul refers to a pre-Christian period. Earlier, in Romans 6 and 7, Paul has written of Christian freedom from sin and from the law. His whole argument would be invalidated "if he now confessed that, at the moment of writing, he was a miserable wretch, a prisoner to sin's law (Rom. 7:24, 23)." Dodd also notes that nothing else in Paul's letters indicates an ongoing struggle of this sort. He concludes that Romans 7 is "an authentic transcript of Paul's own experience during the period which culminated in his vision on the road to Damascus."[48]

Dodd is surely right when he insists that any interpretation of Romans 7 must take its context into account. His own assessment of that context is inadequate, however. This entire section of the letter, Romans 5—8, concerns the problems and promise of *Christian* life. An autobiographical discussion of Paul's conversion would be out of place, both because it concerns an individual believer, and because it deals with a pre-Christian context. Whoever is included in the *egō* is surely a Christian.

Dodd is also right to note that there is no evidence elsewhere that the Christian Paul struggled with guilt and insecurity. But do we have reason to think that Paul experienced a tormented conscience prior to his conversion? Only Dodd's interpretation of this particular text would cause us to see Paul the Pharisee as a man plagued by conscience. Indeed, we gain the opposite impression from Gal. 1:11–17 and especially from Phil. 3:2–11.[49]

A more significant problem with Dodd's argument, as with any argument for understanding Romans 7 as having a pre-Christian reference, is found in vv. 24–25:

> Wretched man that I am! Who will deliver me from this body of death? Thanks be to God through Jesus Christ our Lord! So then, I of myself serve the law of God with my mind, but with my flesh I serve the law of sin.

The last sentence in this text provides a strong, even overwhelming, argument against Dodd's interpretation. If Paul is describing a personal experience of torment which was brought to an end by his encounter with Jesus as Messiah, why does this last sentence appear? Dodd argues that v. 25b logically belongs before vv. 24–25a. He concedes that it is inconceivable that Paul could thank God for his deliverance and then write a concluding self-description which is exactly the same as that found in the earlier verses. Dodd suggests that v. 25b may have been dislocated as the result of a scribal error in the original dictation, or it might have been a marginal comment on vv. 22–23 which was later incorrectly inserted by a copyist.[50]

Dodd's understanding of Romans 7 depends heavily on the hypothesis that 7:25b actually belongs before v. 24, or that it was a scribal comment not included in the original letter, but no textual evidence supports either of these claims. Even if there were such evidence, it would have to appear in reliable early manuscripts in order to support Dodd's argument, since the present text would certainly be regarded as the more difficult and, therefore, the more apt to be early.[51]

For these and other reasons, most New Testament scholars have concluded that, whatever the identity of *egō* in Romans 7, it is not a "transcript" of Paul's "conversion." Many draw on W. G. Kümmel's 1929 monograph, which argued that the *egō* is a stylistic device meaning "one" or "anyone," and concluded that Paul has in mind all persons before Christ or apart from Christ.[52] Others see in the *egō* Paul's present experience as a Christian who has not escaped and cannot escape the perils of living in this age.[53] For our purposes, a precise identification is not significant. What is significant is that Romans 7 does not provide us with information about the conversion of Paul. That conclusion in itself leads us to be extremely wary of interpretations of Paul that contend that while still a persecutor, he experienced some prolonged period of personal questioning, of either a theological or a moral nature.

Conclusions

What has our study of the texts yielded regarding the conversion of Paul? His own statements do not indicate that Paul was tormented by guilt or unhappiness in his early life. Indeed, he claims that he outstripped his peers in religious devotion (Gal. 1:14) and that he was a good and loyal Jew who knew himself to be blameless (Phil. 3:5–6). However, because of an experience of the risen Lord (1 Cor. 9:1–2; 15:8–11), an experience that contained a call to serve as an apostle to Gentiles (Gal. 1:15–16; 1 Cor. 9:1–2; 15:8–10), Paul underwent a radical change. He no longer valued those early credentials (Phil. 3:7); indeed, he regarded them as garbage because of his recognition that Jesus was the Messiah (Phil. 3:8).

By comparison with the familiar narratives of Acts, this description is meager indeed! We find no trip to Damascus as part of an official inquisition, although Damascus is once connected with the conversion (Gal. 1:17; cf. 2 Cor. 11:32). We have here no narration of a miraculous event, no light, no voices, no companions, no blindness. In short, we cannot write about the conversion as the first chapter in a biography of Paul the Christian.

The fact that Paul himself tells us very little about the circumstances of the conversion should not prevent us from understanding the significance of the comments that are given, however. In the first place, Paul consistently leaves the *impression* that this change was sudden and unexpected, although he never says so explicitly or directly. This impression is strongest in Gal. 1:11–17, where Paul shifts abruptly from a description of his earlier life (vv. 15–17). There is no explanation of Paul's thinking, no description of an *event*. Instead, we find a sharp contrast between past and present. The same is true of Philippians 3, where Paul describes himself as having been seized by Christ (v. 12) and, to a lesser extent, of 1 Cor. 15:8–11. If Paul was aware of a prolonged period of searching and questioning, he gives the reader no indication of this struggle.[54]

This abrupt, unexplained change in Paul's life may best be described as a cognitive shift. Paul, both before and after, regarded himself as a good Jew, one whose conduct was exemplary and who maintained the traditions of Judaism. Paul's use of prophetic language in relation to his call indicates that he still saw himself standing within those traditions. His experience meant, however, that his own values and commitments had changed radically. In light of this change, he no longer regarded his earlier accomplishments as worthwhile or significant. That is why we can speak of a shift in cognition: Paul underwent a radical change in his understanding of what made his own life worthwhile. It is for that reason that Paul can say, "Indeed, I count everything as loss . . ." (Phil. 3:8).

This certainly is not to say that Paul's conversion was simply, or even primarily, a change in self-understanding. He makes it clear in the texts we have examined and elsewhere that this event was pivotally messianic:

"[He] was pleased to reveal his son to me . . ." (Gal. 1:16);

"Indeed I count everything as loss because of the surpassing worth of knowing Christ Jesus my Lord" (Phil. 3:8);

"Have I not seen Jesus our Lord?" (1 Cor. 9:1);

"Last of all, as to one untimely born, he appeared also to me" (1 Cor. 15:8).

It was the recognition that Jesus was the Messiah that forced Paul to reject his previous accomplishments in favor of his new vocation as apostle (Gal. 1:15–17) and in favor of being "found in Christ" (Phil. 3:9).[55]

Neither the messianic focus of this change nor its effects upon Paul's own values and commitments can be isolated from the rest of Paul's thought. Paul understood his experience to be paradigmatic of that of every Christian. As his life had been changed, so Paul expected Christians in his churches to understand that they had been called from unworthiness to worthiness (1 Cor. 1:26–31). In Philippians, Paul concludes his discussion of the radical change in his own thinking by imploring the reader to imitate him (Phil. 3:17; cf. 1 Cor. 4:16; 11:1). In Galatians, his own experience introduces a larger argument in which one important thrust is that Christians are "in Christ" and are, therefore, not to exist on the basis of traditional human categories (3:28–29). The Christ event, then, meant that everything was subject to the overwhelming importance of the fact that the Messiah had come and would soon return. This is true both for Paul and for every Christian.[56]

Can we go beyond the few details that Paul gives us and say something more specific about the cause and nature of his conversion? Here we are dealing largely with conjecture. Nevertheless, the recurrence of certain motifs in the texts we have examined *may* indicate those concerns that were central to his change. Of primary interest here is the identity of the Messiah. Since, as we have seen, all of these texts deal with Paul's experience of the Messiah, it is appropriate to conclude that there was something about the church's proclamation of the Messiah that was offensive to Paul before his conversion. He does not explicitly tell us what that offense was, yet the change in values that seems to be closely related to Paul's conversion may indicate that the church's Messiah was, at first, offensive to Paul because of his crucifixion. That is, the claim that one who had been executed was the Messiah was considered by Paul, the protector of Jewish tradition, to be scandalous, and the event that led Paul to change his mind about Jesus also led Paul to change his mind about the crucifixion and his other preconceptions.

But did Paul persecute the church because it proclaimed a crucified Messiah? Even in view of our conclusion that Paul's "persecution" of Christians was probably verbal rather than violent, this motivation seems very unlikely. It is difficult to understand why anyone would "pursue" a group of people simply because they affirmed that a man who had been crucified was the Messiah. It is more probable that, while Paul was offended that a crucified man was being proclaimed the Messiah, his "persecution" of Christians is related to something about the earliest community itself. The strong impression left by the Synoptic tradition is that Jesus and his followers were among those outside the religious and secular power structures (e.g., Mark 2:13–17 and par.; 2:18–22 and par.; 2:23–25 and par.; 7:1–23). It may be that before his conversion Paul was scandalized by the claim that the Messiah had appeared to a group of outcasts, some of whom even lived outside the law.[57] For Paul, whose pride in his status among his people was great, such a claim would have been an extreme offense. Perhaps the offense was extreme enough to cause Paul to lash out publicly against those who made such claims. Paul's rejection of the things that he once regarded as important stems from his conversion, which forced him to acknowledge that God had indeed acted through those whom Paul regarded as unworthy. Hence, Paul's own convictions are again called into question.

I have suggested that there are at least three broad types of change that fall under the heading of conversion: alternation, pendulum-like conversion, and transformation. In addition to these, as noted earlier, it is often argued that Paul experienced a call rather than a conversion. Do any of these types apply to the change to which Paul refers in his letters?

Alternation can be ruled out at once, since Paul's messianic convictions and apostleship do not proceed naturally from his earlier choices! This change is by no means the predictable result of earlier choices. Neither does Paul experience a pendulum-like conversion in which the affirmed present and future require a rejected past. Whatever the relationship between Paul the Pharisee and Paul the apostle, it is not as simple as the pendulum-like change might lead us to believe. Paul does not *reject* the past; rather, it has been *subjected* by the advent of the Messiah. Stendahl and others who employ the word conversion only for a pendulum-like shift are certainly right to deny its applicability to Paul.

Are we well-advised, then, to avoid conversion language and to speak only of Paul's *call*? No. While the term "call" describes one aspect of Paul's change from persecutor to apostle, it does not do justice to the several motifs used by Paul. To speak only of Paul's "call" is to suggest that the texts we have studied have to do only with a commission to a particular role or task. "Call" does not encompass Paul's recognition of Jesus as Messiah or his radical change in values and commitments. The term touches on the change Paul describes, but it is not sufficient to evoke all that is included in those texts.

What Paul describes in his letters is a *transformation*. The revelation of Jesus as Messiah brought about in Paul a transformed understanding of God and God's actions in the world. As in the diagrams of Gestalt psychology, the "picture" Paul has of Jesus, Jesus' followers, and of Paul himself undergoes a radical change. What had once seemed unthinkable—a crucified Messiah—becomes a revelation. What once had seemed to be zealous becomes irrelevant, outdated, passé. To say that the "picture" changed is not to say that the truth had *always* been present. God has done a new thing in the Christ event, but that new thing was at one point hidden from Paul. Paul's own perception of the "picture" had prevented him from seeing what God had done. In the transformation, Paul is able to see the "picture" in a new way.

THE TRANSFORMATION OF BELIEVERS

When we take up the narratives of Acts, we will be interested in how Luke interprets Paul's conversion as well as the conversions of other persons. Before we do that, however, it is important to ask another question about Paul and conversion, namely, how does Paul understand conversion and transformation within the context of the community of believers? How did Paul view the change brought about when people received the gospel? What does such a change involve?

It is important that we be clear about what questions are included here and what questions are excluded. Although Paul's understanding of conversion and transformation necessarily touches on his soteriology, we are not primarily interested in how humanity is saved, from what it is saved, and for what it is saved. We also are not asking about methods employed by Paul and his co-workers in their mission or about steps toward conversion or stages in conversion. Instead, we are asking what indications Paul's letters give regarding his view of conversion and transformation.

A reminder concerning the nature of our sources is appropriate. We do not have transcripts of Paul's sermons. Nor do we have access to what he might have said to persons who responded positively to his sermons and wanted to hear more about the gospel. Nor do we have his homilies, if there were such, to those being baptized. All of the material we have from Paul comes from letters he wrote to particular congregations of believers. While those letters contain a variety of material—hymns, confessions, bits of sermons—we have no direct access to his comments to those who were new believers. We can only ask whether and in what way the letters *reflect* Paul's understanding of conversion and transformation.

We begin with Paul's use of conversion language. That is, we will look at the expressions he employs when referring to reception of the gospel. Then we turn to the concept of transformation as it appears in Rom. 12:1–2 and elsewhere.

Epistrephein and *epistrophē* are conventional terms for "conversion" that appear in the Septuagint and elsewhere.[58] Paul never uses the noun, *epistrophē* (turning, conversion), and he employs the verb, *epistrephein*, in ways quite consistent with convention.

> For they themselves report concerning us what a welcome we had among you, and how you turned *(epistrephein)* to God from idols, to serve a living and true God, and to wait for his Son from heaven, whom he raised from the dead, Jesus who delivers us from the wrath to come. (1 Thess. 1:9–10)

Here Paul describes the reception of the gospel among the Thessalonians. These are not Jews who have recognized in Jesus the Messiah of God, but Gentiles who have turned from the service of the gods to the service of the God of Israel and the Messiah.[59]

> Formerly, when you did not know God, you were in bondage to beings that by nature are not gods; but now that you have come to know God, or rather to be known by God, how can you turn back *(epistrephein)* again to the weak and beggarly elemental spirits, whose slaves you want to be once more? (Gal. 4:8–9)

The conventional meaning of *epistrephein* is used here to make clear to believers in Galatia that their wish to submit to the law of Moses does not mean they will complete the requirements of the gospel, but that they will abandon the gospel. They will have reconverted.[60]

> Yes, to this day whenever Moses is read a veil lies over their minds; but when a man turns *(epistrephein)* to the Lord the veil is removed.[61] (2 Cor. 3:15–16)

The immediate context suggests that, unlike 1 Thess. 1:9–10 and Gal. 4:8–9, Paul here uses *epistrephein* of Jewish Christians. However, a review of the larger context (2 Cor. 2:14—5:21) indicates that Paul addresses not merely the blinding of Israel, but the impact of the gospel on all believers.[62] Figuratively speaking, a veil is removed from Gentiles as well as from Jews, whenever they "turn to the Lord."

Another term frequently associated with conversion in the Greco-Roman world is *metanoun* (to repent, to change one's mind) or *metanoia* (repentance), but Paul seldom speaks of repentance and never characterizes coming to faith as an act of repentance.

> As it is, I rejoice, not because you were grieved, but because you were grieved into repenting *(metanoia)*; for you felt a godly grief, so that you suffered no loss through us. For godly grief produces a repentance *(metanoia)* that leads to salvation and brings no regret, but worldly grief produces death. (2 Cor. 7:9–10)
>
> I fear that when I come again my God may humble me before you, and I may have to mourn over many of those who sinned before and have not repented *(metanoun)* of the impurity, immorality, and licentiousness which they have practiced. (2 Cor. 12:21)
>
> Or do you presume upon the riches of his kindness and forbearance and patience? Do you not know that God's kindness is meant to lead you to repentance *(metanoia)*? (Rom. 2:4)

These are the only places in Paul's letters where either *metanoia* or *metanoun* appears, and in every case he is referring to the repentance of persons who already profess faith in Jesus as Messiah.

Although Paul seldom employs these conventional expressions for conversion, he does occasionally refer in other ways to the point at which persons come to faith. In 1 Corinthians 14, he describes the impact of worship on an outsider (vv. 24–25):

> But if all prophesy, and an unbeliever or outsider enters, he is convicted by all, he is called to account by all, the secrets of his heart are disclosed; and so, falling on his face, he will worship God and declare that God is really among you.

An unbeliever who enters the worship of the community and finds prophecy or true proclamation there will be confronted by the truth of the gospel and will acknowledge God's presence within the community. While this text does not address explicitly the conversion of an outsider, it does give some indication of what precedes that conversion.

At the outset of the same letter, Paul refers to the beginning of faith at Corinth as God's *call*: "For consider your call *(klēsis)*, brethren; not many of you were wise according to worldly standards, not many were powerful, not many were of noble birth . . ." (1 Cor. 1:26). When describing the labor of Apollos and himself, Paul speaks of "servants through whom you believed" (1 Cor. 3:5). Here "to believe" *(pisteuein)* has the connotation of entering into faith (cf. 1 Cor. 15:1–2; Rom. 13:11).[63]

Romans 6 describes conversion as a process of liberation and enslavement (vv. 17–18):

> But thanks be to God, that you who were once slaves of sin have become obedient from the heart to the standard of teaching to which you were committed, and having been set free from sin, have become slaves of righteousness.

Clearly no one expression automatically appears when Paul has reason to refer to the movement of a person or a community to faith. It is even arguable that the texts noted above do not refer to a point in time or a crisis of decision. On the whole, it must be admitted that Paul's letters evidence almost a complete lack of interest in either the process or the act of conversion. The handful of texts that may refer to conversion only underscore this point. As odd as it may seem, the apostle to the Gentiles has little to say about the way in which those Gentiles become believers.

Paul's virtual silence on this topic merits some reflection, since even what is *not* said may tell us a great deal. We need, first, to recall what has been noted above about the nature of the sources. Paul wrote to persons who had already become part of "all those who in every place call on the name of our Lord Jesus Christ" (1 Cor. 1:2). His letters are not missionary tracts or instructions for new converts. Instead, they address the problems of those who are already "in Christ."

Paul's silence on the topic of conversion does not stem entirely from the character of his letters, however. Indeed, the very structure of his theology militates against the use of conventional conversion language. *Epistrephein* and *metanoun* most often connote the action of one who changes his or her convictions and thus turns to God (e.g., 1 Thess. 1:9–10; 2 Cor. 12:21). In this mindset, a person acts to rectify the relationship with God. But in Paul's letters it is made clear over and over again that God is the one who acts to include believers.

For Paul, God's act in Christ reveals the sinful condition of all human beings and manifests God's grace for the overcoming of that condition (e.g., Rom. 3:21–26).[64] Thus, when Paul has reason to speak about the beginning of faith, he does so by reference to God's action rather than to human action: God calls (1 Cor. 1:2, 9, 26; Gal. 1:6), God purchases (1 Cor. 6:20; 7:23), God grants grace (Rom. 3:21–26), God liberates (Rom. 6:17–18). Given Paul's overwhelming emphasis on the initiative of God, the absence of conventional conversion language is understandable. It is not believers who turn, but God who turns believers as God "has begun to reclaim for himself the world which belongs to him."[65]

This is not to exclude a human response to God's action. Most often, Paul describes the response as faith, of course. Those whom God has called see in the cross neither foolishness nor weakness but the powerful revelation of God. They understand that the cross signals the end of all established systems of pleasing God and evaluating human beings. And they have confidence that God's power, manifested in God's triumph over death in the resurrection of Jesus, will ultimately prevail over all other powers and authorities.

The impact of this faith or confidence, which is granted by God, is to bring about not merely the conversion of believers but their transformation. Paul does not ask that people repent and turn around, but that they acknowledge God's new creation (Gal. 6:15; 2 Cor. 5:17) and allow themselves to be appropriated by it. Nowhere is this clearer than in Rom. 12:2: "Do not be conformed to this world, but be transformed by the renewal of your mind. . . ." Believers are not to be bound by the shape of this age (Greek, *aiōn*). Because they have renewed minds—or renewed mindsets, in the contemporary idiom— they can *be* transformed.[66] As a result of that transformation, believers are able to discern (*dokimazein*) God's will (12:2b) and are empowered to present to God their entire selves (12:1).

We should not imagine that transformation is, in Paul's view, an event that may be completed. An awkward but literal translation of *metamorphousthe* in Rom. 12:2 is "[you] be being transformed." Transformation continues. While some real and significant change occurs for believers, that change is never finished or complete. Indeed, while Paul can say of himself and of all believers, "It is no longer I who live, but Christ who lives in me" (Gal. 2:20), he also says, "Not that I have already obtained this or am already perfect; but I press on to make it my own, because Christ Jesus has made me his own" (Phil. 3:12).[67]

Up to this point it would appear that Paul's view of transformation has to do entirely with the individual believer, and it is certainly true that Paul addresses the calling and transforming of the individual.[68] Indeed, it is only by virtue of the radical transformation of the cross that the individual is freed from the enslavement of the cosmos and enabled to become an individual.[69] The individual believer does not exist in isolation, apart from the community, however. This is particularly clear in the Corinthian correspondence, because some of the Corinthians understood their freedom to mean that each individual had been authorized to do as he or she pleased. Paul over and over argues against this individualized interpretation of transformation (e.g., 1 Cor. 5:1–8; 8:7–13; 12:12–26). Being baptized into the body of Christ means that each individual is transformed, but it also means that the community as a whole is transformed, or is in the process of being transformed.

To be transformed is to enter into a relationship of interdependence with other believers. Such interdependence emerges in passages like Rom. 15:1–7 and Gal. 6:1–6. Citing the behavior of Christ who did not please himself, Paul urges Roman Christians to seek the upbuilding of the entire fellowship (15:1–3), and he prays that they will be enabled to think the same things, to think as a community (15:5–6). In the same vein, he admonishes the Galatians to be involved in the burdens and cares of one another (6:1–6). The "law of Christ" is fulfilled when believers bear each other's burdens.[70] These pleas are not to be separated from the call to individual transformation, but are part of that transformation. The individual who is transformed is transformed *into* a community of mutual responsibility and commitment.

NOTES

1. Flannery O'Connor, *The Habit of Being,* ed. Sally Fitzgerald (New York: Vintage Books, 1979), 355.

2. This method is often commended by scholars but seldom fully observed. For a review of the ways in which Paul's conversion has been interpreted, see Beverly Roberts Gaventa, *Paul's Conversion: A Critical Sifting of the Epistolary Evidence* (Ann Arbor, Mich.: University Microfilms No. 7905353, 1978), 6–114. Much of the material in the present chapter is developed there in more detail.

3. Stendahl, *Paul Among Jews and Gentiles,* 7–23.

4. F.F. Bruce, *Paul: Apostle of the Heart Set Free* (Grand Rapids: Wm. B. Eerdmans, 1977), 15–16.

5. Ibid., 69–75, 87, 188.

6. Seyoon Kim, *The Origin of Paul's Gospel* (Grand Rapids: Wm. B. Eerdmans, 1981).

7. J. Christiaan Beker, *Paul the Apostle: The Triumph of God in Life and Thought* (Philadelphia: Fortress Press, 1980), ix.

8. Ibid., 3–5.

9. Ibid., 6.

10. Ibid., 9.

11. Billy Graham, *How to Be Born Again* (Waco, Tex.: Word Books, 1977), 152.

12. In both 1 Cor. 9:1–2 and 1 Cor. 15:8–11, Paul says that he saw the Lord and connects that vision with his apostleship. 2 Cor. 4:6 is also sometimes understood to refer to the change Paul experienced. Similarly, it has occasionally been suggested that the experience described in 2 Cor. 12:1–4 is Paul's "conversion." For further discussion and bibliography, see Gaventa, *Paul's Conversion,* 115–94.

13. On Paul's use of *gnōrizō,* see Ernest Dewitt Burton, *A Critical and Exegetical Commentary on the Epistle to the Galatians,* ICC (Edinburgh:

T. & T. Clark, 1921), 35; M. J. Lagrange, *Saint Paul Epitre aux Galater* (Paris: J. Gabalda et Cie, 1950), 9; D. Albrecht Oepke, *Der Brief des Paulus an die Galater,* THKNT 9, 3d ed. rev. (Berlin: Evangelische Verlagsanstalt, 1973), 54; Pierre Bonnard, *L'epitre de Saint Paul aux Galates,* CNT 9, 2d ed. (Neuchatel, Switzerland: Delachaux & Niestle, 1972), 27.

14. Joachim Jeremias, *"anthrōpos,"* TDNT 1:364; Hans Lietzmann, *An die Galater,* HNT, 4th ed. (Tübingen: J. C. B. Mohr [Paul Siebeck], 1971), 6.

15. Oscar Cullmann, *The Early Church: Studies in Early Christian History and Theology,* ed. A. J. B. Higgins (Philadelphia: Westminster Press, 1956), 60–69.

16. For a more complete discussion of this issue, see William Baird, "What is the Kerygma? A Study of 1 Cor. 15:3–8 and Gal. 1:11–17," *JBL* 76 (1957): 189–91; W. D. Davies, *The Setting of the Sermon on the Mount* (Cambridge: Cambridge Univ. Press, 1966), 355–62; J. H. Schütz, *Paul and the Anatomy of Apostolic Authority,* SNTSMS 26 (Cambridge: Cambridge Univ. Press, 1975), 54–58.

17. On the early development of traditions about the apostles, see Jacob Jervell, *Luke and the People of God* (Minneapolis: Augsburg Pub. House, 1972), 19–39.

18. It does appear in Eph. 4:22; 1 Tim. 4:12; Heb. 13:7; James 3:13; 1 Pet. 1:15; in each case it refers to conduct appropriate to a Christian.

19. It occurs in the New Testament only here. Outside of the texts noted, it appears nowhere in the Greek Old Testament, the Apocrypha, the Pseudepigrapha, Philo, or Josephus.

20. Martin Hengel, *Judaism and Hellenism,* 2 vols., trans. John Bowden (Philadelphia: Fortress Press; London: SCM Press, 1974), 1:1–2.

21. Oepke, *An die Galater,* 30; Donald Guthrie, *Galatians* (London: Thomas Nelson & Sons, 1969), 67.

22. On *hyperbolē,* see BAGD, 840; Arland Hultgren, "Paul's Pre-Christian Persecution of the Church," *JBL* 95 (1976): 108–9.

23. Elsewhere Paul uses *diōkein* seventeen times, eight of which refer to a nonviolent pursuit of some goal (Rom. 9:30, 31; 12:13; 14:19; 1 Cor. 14:1; Phil. 3:12), and nine of which are ambiguous (Rom. 12:14; 1 Cor. 4:12; 15:19; 2 Cor. 4:9; Gal. 1:23; 4:29; 5:11; 6:12; Phil. 3:6). Paul uses *porthein* only here and in Gal. 1:23. Its usage elsewhere consistently connotes material or moral ruin or violence. On this see Philippe H. Menoud, "Le sens du verbe *porthein* (Gal. 1:13, 23; Acts 9:21)," *Apophoreta: Festschrift für Ernst Haenchen,* ed. F. H. Kettler, BZNW 30 (Berlin: Verlag Alfred Töpelmann, 1964), 178–86.

24. On the influence of Acts, see Menoud, "Le sens du verbe *porthein,"* 180–82. Douglas R. A. Hare studied the problem of Jewish persecution of Christians and concluded that most such persecution took the form of informal social ostracism and economic boycott. He found little evidence for execution, flogging, or imprisonment (*The Theme of Jewish Persecution of*

Christians in the Gospel According to St. Matthew, SNTSMS 6 [Cambridge: Cambridge Univ. Press, 1967], 59–60, 77–79).

25. Useful here is the study of zeal by David M. Rhoads in *Israel in Revolution 6–74 C.E.: A Political History Based on the Writings of Josephus* (Philadelphia: Fortress Press, 1976), 84–87.

26. See also LXX Judg. 13:5; Ps. 22[21]:10; 58[57]:3; 71[70]:6; F. F. Bruce, *The Epistle to the Galatians,* NIGTC (Grand Rapids: Wm. B. Eerdmans, 1981), 92.

27. See, e.g., 1 Sam. 2:27; 3:7, 21a; 2 Sam. 7:27a; Amos 3:7; Dan. 2:19, 22, 28–30. This is not at all to suggest that *apokalyptein* in the LXX always has this meaning; indeed, it is very often used in a literal sense or for the disclosure of a secret or an injustice.

28. For further discussion, see Gaventa, *Paul's Conversion,* 233–36.

29. Oepke, *An die Galater,* 60–61 (also *"en,"* *TDNT 2:539*); Mussner, *Der Galaterbrief,* HTKNT (Freiburg: Herder, 1974), 86; BAGD, 261; BDF, 118; J. H. Moulton, ed., *A Grammar of New Testament Greek,* 4 vols. (Edinburgh: T. & T. Clark, 1906–76), vol. 3: *Syntax,* Nigel Turner (1963), 264; C. F. D. Moule, *Idiom Book of New Testament Greek* (Cambridge: Cambridge Univ. Press, 1959), 76.

30. Again, the language is prophetic; cf. Isa. 49:6b and Jer. 1:5.

31. The literary integrity of Philippians is assumed here; see Gaventa, *Paul's Conversion,* 247–54.

32. Ibid., 254–58.

33. Paul's use of the term *Israel* is difficult, particularly in Gal. 6:16 and Rom. 11:26. On this, see W. D. Davies, "Paul and the People of Israel," *NTS* 24 (1977): 4–39.

34. Marvin R. Vincent, *A Critical and Exegetical Commentary on the Epistles to the Philippians and to Philemon,* ICC (Edinburgh: T. & T. Clark, 1897), 96; R. P. Martin, *The Epistle of Paul to the Philippians,* Tyndale New Testament Commentaries (Grand Rapids: Wm. B. Eerdmans, 1959), 142; G. B. Caird, *Paul's Letters from Prison* (London: Oxford Univ. Press, 1976), 135.

35. Jean Collange, *L'epitre de Saint Paul aux Philippiens,* CNT (Neuchatel: Delachaux et Niestle, 1973), 112 [ET: *The Epistle of St. Paul to the Philippians* (London: Epworth Press, 1979)].

36. On this problem, see J. A. Fitzmyer, "The Languages of Palestine in the First Century A.D.," *CBQ* 32 (1970): 518–28.

37. E.g., Philo, *On the Confusion of Tongues* 68.129, *The Life of Moses* 2.31–32; Josephus, *Antiquities* 1.36; 4.323.

38. Jacob Neusner, "Pharisaic Law in New Testament Times," *Union Seminary Quarterly Review* 26 (1971): 331–40; idem, *From Politics to Piety: The Emergence of Pharisaic Judaism* (Englewood Cliffs, N.J.: Prentice-Hall, 1973).

39. Those who see a necessary connection between the two include Collange (*Philippiens,* 112), and Caird (*Paul's Letters from Prison,* 136).

40. Vincent, *Philippians and Philemon*, 99; Martin Dibelius, *An die Thessalonicher I–II. An die Philipper*, HNT, 2d ed. (Tübingen: J. C. B. Mohr [Paul Siebeck], 1925), 68; F. W. Beare, *A Commentary on the Epistle to the Philippians*, HNTC (New York: Harper & Brothers, 1959), 109; Martin, *Philippians*, 143.

41. *Skybalon*, which occurs only here in the New Testament, can mean refuse, rubbish, or dung (Sir. 27:4; Josephus, *War* 5.571; see BAGD, 758).

42. Beker quite rightly warns against a mystical or sentimental view of the cross (*Paul the Apostle*, 199).

43. F. C. Porter, *The Mind of Christ in Paul* (New York: Charles Scribner's Sons, 1930), 215–16; Collange, *Philippiens*, 111.

44. Stendahl, *Paul Among Jews and Gentiles*, 78–96.

45. Robert Gundry argues that the *egō* refers to Paul's pre-Christian difficulty with the prohibition concerning lust, but Gundry distinguishes that view from the notion that what we have in Romans 7 describes "the decisive element" in Paul's "conversion." ("The Moral Frustration of Paul Before His Conversion: Sexual Lust in Romans 7:7–25," *Pauline Studies*, ed. D. A. Hagner and M. J. Harris [Grand Rapids: Wm. B. Eerdmans, 1980], 228–45).

46. Gaventa, *Paul's Conversion*, 315.

47. C. H. Dodd, *The Epistle of Paul to the Romans*, MNTC (New York: Ray Long and Richard R. Smith, 1932), 104–7, 111.

48. Ibid., 107–8.

49. On this, see Stendahl, *Paul Among Jews and Gentiles*, 78–96; E. P. Sanders, *Paul and Palestinian Judaism: A Comparison of Patterns of Religion* (Philadelphia: Fortress Press, 1977), 443–44.

50. Dodd, *Romans*, 114–15. The suggestion that there is some textual disruption here is also made by Friedrich Müller, "Zwei Manginalien im Brief des Paulus an die Romer," *ZNW* 40 (1941): 249–54; Otto Michel, *Der Brief an die Römer*, 12th ed. (Göttingen: Vandenhoeck & Ruprecht, 1963), 179; and Matthew Black, *Romans*, NCB (Grand Rapids: Wm. B. Eerdmans; London: Marshall, Morgan & Scott, 1973), 108. Others have regarded 7:25b as a gloss: Rudolf Bultmann, "Glossen im Römerbrief," *Theologische Literaturzeitung* 72 (1947): 199; Ulrich Luz, *Das Geschichtsverstandnis des Paulus* (Munich: Kaiser, 1968), 160; Ernst Käsemann, *An die Römer*, HNT (Tübingen: J. C. B. Mohr [Paul Siebeck], 1973), 203 [ET: *Commentary on Romans* (Grand Rapids: Wm. B. Eerdmans, 1980)].

51. So C. K. Barrett, *The Epistle to the Romans*, HNTC (New York: Harper & Row, 1973), 151; C. E. B. Cranfield, *A Critical and Exegetical Commentary on the Epistle to the Romans*, ICC, 2 vols. (Edinburgh: T. & T. Clark, 1975), 1:368–69.

52. W. G. Kümmel, *Römer 7 und das Bild des Menschen im Neuen Testament* (Munich: Chr. Kaiser, 1974 [1929]).

53. For the various interpretations, see Cranfield, *Romans*, 1:342–47.

54. We must bear in mind, of course, that what we have in all these

remarks is retrospection. That is, we have Paul's later interpretation of earlier perceptions and experiences.

55. The central role of the identity of the Messiah, together with the consistent references to Paul's apostleship, is stressed by Sanders, *Paul and Palestinian Judaism*, 441–42.

56. I have explored the paradigmatic function of this text more extensively in an essay not yet published, "Galatians 1 and 2: Autobiography as Paradigm."

57. This suggestion is consistent with the position taken by Martin Dibelius, *Paul*, ed. W. G. Kümmel, trans. F. Clarke (Philadelphia: Westminster Press, 1953), 47–51; W. D. Davies, *Invitation to the New Testament* (Garden City, N.Y.: Doubleday & Co., 1966), 260–63; M. S. Enslin, *Reapproaching Paul* (Philadelphia: Westminster Press, 1972), 56–57.

58. LXX Deut. 30:2. 1 Sam. 7:3; 1 Kings 8:33; Tob. 14:6; Isa. 6:10; Jer. 24:7; Joel 2:12–14; Zech. 1:3; Mal. 3:18; Sir. 5:7; 17:25; Josephus, *Antiquities* 10:53; Philo, *On Joseph* 87, *On the Unchangeableness of God* 17, *On the Confusion of Tongues* 131, *On Dreams* 2.174, *On the Special Laws* 2.256; Epictetus 2.20, 22.

59. The description of Israel's God as a living god, in contrast to the gods worshiped by Gentiles, appears in texts associated with proselytes to Judaism, e.g., *Bel and the Dragon* 5, 25; *Joseph and Asenath* 8.6–8.

60. I cannot agree with Dieter Georgi's characterization of Gal. 4:9 as sarcastic (*Die Geschichte der Kollekte des Paulus für Jerusalem* [Hamburg: Herbert Reich, 1965], 36). Paul has already described the Galatians as turning from God to "another" gospel (1:16), which suggests that what they contemplate is viewed by Paul as a kind of conversion.

61. This verse alludes to Exod. 34:34 ("But whenever Moses went in before the Lord to speak with him, he took the veil off, until he came out . . . "), but Paul introduces the term *epistrephein* for his own purposes (so Bertram, *"epistrephō," TDNT* 7:728).

62. On this text, see J. L. Martyn, "Epistemology at the Turn of the Ages: 2 Corinthians 5:16," in *Christian History and Interpretation: Studies Presented to John Knox*, ed. W. R. Farmer, C. F. D. Moule, R. R. Niebuhr (Cambridge: Cambridge Univ. Press, 1967), 269–87.

63. See also 1 Cor. 15:11; on this use of *pisteuein*, see Sanders, *Paul and Palestinian Judaism*, 463.

64. On this issue, see W. D. Davies, "From Tyranny to Liberation: The Pauline Experience of Alienation and Reconciliation," in *Jewish and Pauline Studies* (Philadelphia: Fortress Press, 1984), 189–244.

65. Ernst Käsemann, "Worship and Everyday Life: A Note on Romans 12," in *New Testament Questions of Today*, trans. W. J. Montague (Philadelphia: Fortress Press, 1969), 189.

66. For a thorough discussion of this motif in Paul, consult John T. Koenig,

"The Motif of Transformation in the Pauline Epistles: A History-of-Religions/Exegetical Study" (Ph.D. diss., Union Theological Seminary, 1970).

67. "Conversion is a decisive event of the past—there is no question on that score so far as Paul is concerned. But this certainly does not mean that the believer's old nature (attitudes, values, desires, etc.) are dead, or that he is dead to them—very much to the contrary. The dying of the old nature and the dying to the old nature is *a life-long process* which will not be completed till the death or transformation of the body" (J. D. G. Dunn, *Jesus and the Spirit* [Philadelphia: Westminster Press 1975], 335).

68. The classic description of this feature of Paul's thought remains that of Rudolf Bultmann in his *Theology of the New Testament*, trans. K. Grobel, 2 vols. (New York: Charles Scribner's Sons, 1951), 1:185–352. See also the penetrating response of Ernst Käsemann, "On Paul's Anthropology," *Perspectives on Paul*, trans. M. Kohl (Philadelphia: Fortress Press, 1971), 1–31.

69. Käsemann, "On Paul's Anthropology," 31.

70. On this extremely difficult text, see the work of Richard B. Hays, "Christology and Ethics in Galatians: The Law of Christ," *CBQ* (forthcoming).

CHAPTER 2

"Why Do You
Persecute Me?"

Conversion in
Luke-Acts (Part 1)

The examination of the letters of Paul in chapter 1 yielded little information about a "conversion event." The few texts that refer to Paul's transformation reflect a radical change, perhaps also a sudden change, in perspective and commitments. Clearly this change revolved around Paul's acknowledgment of the messiahship of Jesus ("when he chose to reveal his Son to me" [Gal. 1:16]; "on account of Christ" [Phil. 3:7]). There are, however, no details about a conversion event; indeed, it is doubtful that the word "event" is even applicable.

By contrast, Luke[1] includes in the second half of his work three accounts of the conversion of Paul. That repetition in itself suggests that Luke understands this matter to be of major significance. Not only is the story repeated, but it is told in such a compelling way that it has become far more familiar to Christians than the brief comments in the epistles. After all, it is Luke's narration to which people refer when they speak of a Damascus road experience.

The subtitle of this chapter, "Conversion in Luke-Acts (Part 1)," indicates the nature of the task at hand. We want to look back to chapter 1 in order to compare Luke with the letters on the matter of Paul's conversion, but we also want to look ahead to chapter 3 and ask what the conversion narratives indicate concerning Luke's understanding of conversion in general. Does Luke-Acts reflect a clear and systematic view of how one becomes a Christian and what that change means? Is Paul a model, a paradigmatic convert? Or is he, on the contrary, so unusual that the narratives about his conversion have no place in a discussion of Luke's understanding of conversion?

When addressing these questions, it will also be necessary to study the accounts in and of themselves. How do they describe Paul and his conversion? How are they related to the immediate context? What function or functions do these narratives have in the larger work? What is their significance for Luke?

These are not, of course, new questions. Owing to enormous interest in Paul and to the unique place of the Acts of the Apostles in the canon, the accounts of Paul's conversion have been examined over and over again. More often than not, however, students of the New Testament have isolated the three Lukan accounts from their narrative context, compared them with one another and with the Pauline letters, and then drawn conclusions about their origin and history, giving slight if any attention to the contexts in which the narratives appear.

A brief review of the study of Acts during the last century will confirm this observation. While scholars were still preoccupied with using Acts to reconstruct the history of the early church, they simply harmonized the accounts in Acts with Paul's own comments to produce the history of Paul's conversion.[2] Among the most pronounced efforts are those from scholars who, influenced by the new psychoanalytic movement, read Romans 7 into the Acts accounts and produced the history of Paul's internal conflict and its climax on the Damascus road.[3]

During the early part of this century, scholarly preoccupation with source analysis led to theories about the sources behind the accounts in Acts 9, 22, and 26. Emanuel Hirsch, for example, explained the variations among the accounts by arguing that Acts 9 is from a Damascus source, Acts 26 is from Paul himself, and Acts 22 is Luke's synthesis of these two sources. Thus, any discrepancies among the accounts were ascribed to the presence of multiple sources rather than to the demands of a particular context.[4]

Since the publication of Hans Conzelmann's *The Theology of St. Luke*, students of Luke-Acts have primarily been concerned to understand Lukan theology. As a result, investigators have used the narratives of Paul's conversion as a mine of information about Luke's understanding of Paul and his significance in relation to the Twelve. Two of the more recent contributions to this aspect of Lukan study have come at the problem by separating pre-Lukan material from Lukan redaction, an effort designed to ascertain Luke's view of Paul more accurately. Christoph Burchard, for example, argues that Acts 9 stands closer to early tradition than do Acts 22 and 26 because Acts 9 portrays the event as a conversion instead of a call. Burchard goes on to suggest that Luke rewrote the material in Acts 9 in order to produce the accounts of Acts 22 and 26.[5] Although Karl Löning comes to very different conclusions about the Lukan Paul, he also understands Acts 9 to be early material, contending that the accounts in 22 and 26 are apologies and as such they would not have stood in early tradition.[6] While both Burchard and Löning make significant contributions to our understandings of the texts, neither deals seriously with the context of the conversion narratives.

By beginning with the assumption that the traditions behind Luke can be isolated, neither asks the pivotal question, whether Acts 9 differs from Acts 22 and 26 because of something intrinsic to the story that Luke wishes to tell. As we turn now to that story, our goal is to understand the accounts of Paul's conversion themselves, with attention to their separate contexts, before making any effort to seek out traditional materials or to compare Acts with Paul.

ACTS 9

At this point, as at many points in reading the New Testament, modern readers are at a distinct disadvantage. We know so well the way the story unfolds that we have difficulty setting aside our knowledge in order to read or hear the narrative on its own terms. Our acquaintance with the whole of Luke-Acts, the epistles, the secondary literature, and a good deal of novelistic tradition stays with us and colors our understanding of the story Luke tells.

For example, the familiarity of Acts 9 may prevent our asking why Luke introduces Paul at precisely this juncture. Paul's missionary work begins in earnest quite a bit later (11:25–26). More important, Luke is in the middle of describing the movement of the church out from Jerusalem and will shortly take up the conversion of Cornelius and its implications (10:1—11:18). Why pause here to tell the story of Paul? Familiarity may also lead us to assume that Paul's activity as a persecutor is explained in some detail or that his call to preach is narrated. While a fresh reading is difficult to achieve, it may reveal a number of interesting aspects of the story.

Paul (or Saul) first appears at 7:58, the stoning of Stephen. Luke calls him simply "a young man" *(neanias)*. No other word of introduction explains his background or motives. Gradually, however, the role of Saul emerges. In 7:58b he is merely a bystander at whose feet the participants place their garments. Immediately following this introduction we read the final words of Stephen and the account of his death. Then comes the second reference to Saul: "Saul was consenting to his death" (8:1). Now Saul approves the action against Stephen, although he is still not an active participant. His activity begins in 8:3, in connection with the "great persecution," when Saul emerges as a major figure who rages against the church by entering homes and taking people off to prison. Lest we miss the full impact of this, Luke places a final word about Stephen just before Saul's emergence as an active persecutor: "Devout men buried Stephen, and made great lamentation over him. But Saul was ravaging the church, and entering house after house, he dragged off men and women and committed them to prison" (8:2–3).[7]

This is not the only connection Luke makes between Stephen and Saul. Stephen's concluding accusations in 7:51–53 announce the action of the mob that kills him, but Saul's activity as persecutor also fulfills Stephen's words. The verb "persecute" *(diōkein)* which appears in the question, "Which of the prophets did your fathers not persecute?" reappears, and indeed dominates, the encounter of Saul with Jesus in 9:4 and 5 ("Why do you persecute me? . . . I am Jesus whom you persecute"). Stephen describes his enemies as murderers *(phoneis)*, and Paul breathes "threat and murder" *(phonos)* in 9:1. Beyond these verbal echoes of 7:51–53 is the parallel between the spirit of resistance described by Stephen and that acted out by Saul in 8:3 and 9:1–2.

This foreshadowing of Saul and his story does not end with Stephen's accusations. In 7:60, between the introduction of Saul and the description of his concurrence with the murder of Stephen, Luke describes Stephen's final words: "Do not hold this sin against them." While this cry first refers to those who have acted against Stephen, it also announces the "forgiveness" of Saul which Luke portrays in Acts 9.

From our point of view, Luke's introduction of Saul is less than satisfying. He tells nothing of Saul's background, education, or motives. Although Saul will later describe himself as "zealous" (22:3), here we learn only one thing: Saul is the enemy.[8] Luke places him among others who persecuted the prophets and contrasts him with the pious people who bury Stephen. Such devices only underscore the seriousness of the charge. We understand that Saul is the enemy and, when he reappears in Acts 9, we will expect further difficulties for believers.

Because of the persecution that breaks out in Jerusalem, believers flee the city, and thus begins the preaching of the gospel in Samaria and the acceptance of the gospel by those outside the bounds of Jerusalem Judaism (8:4–40). The joy with which the Ethiopian eunuch goes on his way stands in sharp contrast to the hostile description of Saul, who is reintroduced in 9:1.[9]

The story beginning in 9:1 represents the best of Luke's narrative art. There are five distinct scenes: (1) the persecution that leads Saul to Damascus (vv. 1–2), (2) the encounter with Jesus and its results (vv. 3–9), (3) the commission of Ananias (vv. 10–16), (4) the action of Ananias and its results (vv. 17–19a), (5) the epilogue (vv. 19b–30).[10]

Scene 1

> But Saul, still breathing threats and murder against the disciples of the Lord, went to the high priest and asked him for letters to the synagogues at Damascus, so that if he found any belonging to the Way, men or women, he might bring them bound to Jerusalem. (Acts 9:1–2)

Scene 1 looks both backward to Saul's introduction and forward to the decisive encounter that begins in v. 3. Luke explains that Saul is "still" persecuting the church. Indeed, what Luke says is that Saul is still "breathing threat and murder" (cf. 7:52).[11] His objects are the "disciples of the Lord." Although we find *mathētēs* (disciple) twenty-eight times in Acts, and seven of those times are in this chapter, this is the only place in which the qualification *tou kyriou* (of the Lord) occurs. The contrast noted earlier between Saul and Stephen now becomes a contrast between Saul and the *Lord's* disciples.

Saul's activity takes on a specific form in v. 2, when he seeks from the high priest official authorization to pursue believers into Damascus. This movement outside Jerusalem escalates Saul's persecution one final step. If the preaching of the disciples is no longer confined to Jerusalem (8:4–40), the same is true of their persecution.[12] Nevertheless, Jerusalem remains the center of authority since those whom Saul locates are to be brought back to Jerusalem (cf. 8:14–15).

The stage is now set for the encounter of scene 2. Even now, all we know about Saul is that he persecuted the church. We learn nothing concerning his motives or his goals. The statement that he sought letters from the high priest indicates primarily that he actively shaped the persecution, and that yet another, more advanced, stage of persecution has begun. All we can say about him is that he is the enemy of believers.

Scene 2

> Now as he journeyed he approached Damascus, and suddenly a light from heaven flashed about him. And he fell to the ground and heard a voice saying to him, "Saul, Saul, why do you persecute me?" And he said, "Who are you, Lord?" And he said, "I am Jesus, whom you are persecuting; but rise and enter the city, and you will be told what you are to do." The men who were traveling with him stood speechless, hearing the voice but seeing no one. Saul arose from the ground; and when his eyes were opened, he could see nothing; so they led him by the hand and brought him into Damascus. And for three days he was without sight, and neither ate nor drank. (Acts 9:3–9)

As the enemy, Saul sets out for Damascus. The repetition of v. 3 emphasizes that Saul's encounter occurs while he is still en route: "But while he was going it happened as he drew near to Damascus" (au. trans.). Either "while going" or "as he drew near to Damascus" would have been sufficient indication that Paul was still on his journey; the presence of both phrases underscores the time.[13]

Verse 3b describes an abrupt interruption in Saul's journey: "Suddenly around him shone a light from heaven" (au. trans.). Saul's response, falling to the earth, acknowledges that some extraordinary event has begun. Here the language is reminiscent of descriptions of hearing God's voice in the Septuagint (cf. Num. 7:89; Isa. 6:8). What Saul hears begins with the double vocative which is familiar from the OT:

> But the angel of the Lord called to him from heaven, and said, "Abraham! Abraham!" And he said, "Here am I." (Gen. 22:11)
>
> And God spoke to Israel in visions of the night, and said, "Jacob, Jacob." And he said, "Here am I." (Gen. 46:2)
>
> God called to him out of the bush, "Moses, Moses!" And he said, "Here am I." (Exod. 3:4)
>
> Then the Lord called, "Samuel! Samuel!" And he said, "Here am I!" (1 Sam. 3:4, cf. 3:10)

Following the double vocative comes the question that epitomizes the work of Saul: "Why do you persecute me?" *Diōkein*, the verb here translated "persecute," seldom occurs in Luke-Acts apart from its connection with Paul (Luke 11:49; 17:23; 21:12; Acts 7:52). Saul is, for Luke, the *one* who deserves that title (Acts 22:4, 7, 8; 26:11, 14, 15).[14]

Saul's response in v. 5a, itself a question, enhances the drama of this conversation in two ways. First, it sets up a situation in which the identity of the speaker must be stated explicitly and in which the accusation against Saul may be repeated. It also introduces a note of irony. Saul addresses the speaker as *kyrios*, which may mean either the worshipful "lord" or simply the polite "sir." Because the question itself indicates that Saul does not know the identity of the one who has spoken, it seems that the latter is intended. Saul will soon, however, regard this speaker as "lord," and Luke's introduction of *kyrios* here points ahead to that time.

The response to Saul's question is emphatic: "I am Jesus whom you persecute" (v. 5b). Both pronouns are emphatic, heightening the distance between Jesus and Saul, and underscoring the importance of this statement. Ernst Haenchen rightly connects this with Luke 10:16, "He who rejects you, rejects me."[15]

Notice that our understanding of Saul's role remains the same. He is still presented exclusively as the persecutor. What is new here is the identification of Jesus as the object of Saul's persecution. All that Saul has been involved in now has its proper title: persecutor of Jesus.

No further explanation from Jesus or question from Saul is given. Instead, we read a simple command: "But rise and enter the city, and you will be told what you are to do" (v. 6). In the single word, *but*, stands the disjuncture between Saul the enemy and the new figure who emerges from this event.[16]

Verse 6 alters the encounter from an accusation to a commission. "Rise and enter" reflects once more the language of the Septuagint, where *anistēmi* frequently introduces divine commissions (e.g., Gen. 21:18; 31:13; 1 Kings 17:9; Jon. 1:2). Although the commission itself is not specified, v. 6b announces that there will be one: "It will be told to you what it is necessary for you to do" (au. trans.). The presence of "it is necessary" *(dei),* which Luke frequently connects with the fulfillment of prophecy,[17] indicates that Saul will not only become a believer, but that he will have some particular role (cf. Luke 21:9; 22:37; 24:26; Acts 1:16; 17:3; 19:21; 23:11). Commentators sometimes maintain that Luke mentions Saul's commission only in vv. 13–16, if at all, but already v. 6b hints at what is to come.

With the announcement that Saul will be told what he must do, the encounter closes. It is clear that the scene, which identifies Saul's activity and brings it to an abrupt halt, forms one of the major turning points of the narrative of Acts. The crescendo of Luke's portrait of Saul the enemy has stopped. Verses 7–9, as we will see, have a transitional function. They underscore the importance of the encounter by emphasizing its results. Verses 7–9 also set the stage for Ananias's role by describing Saul's blindness.

Verse 7 mentions Saul's companions for the first time. They "stood speechless, hearing the voice but seeing no one." Because Acts 22:9 and 26:14 describe this behavior in a slightly different way, many have devoted much attention to the discrepancies among the three accounts. While these discrepancies ought not be glossed over, and I shall make some comments on them below, there is a more immediate question. That is, what is the relationship between the experience of the companions and that of Saul? We read that they are speechless, they hear a voice, but they see no one. We read also that Saul hears a voice, but nothing is said about whether Saul sees someone. Are we to assume that he saw Jesus, or are we to think that his experience was like that of his companions? In other words, do the companions have the function of corroborating Saul's experience, or do they stand in contrast to Saul?

It may well be that this is one of those questions for which there is no answer. There are, however, some indications that the companions stand in contrast to Saul. They underscore the importance of the encounter because their own experience is so different. When Luke says that they do not see anyone, the verb used is *theōrein*, a verb which in Luke-Acts frequently appears in connection with seeing some manifestation of God's activity (e.g., Luke 10:18; 24:37, 39; Acts 3:16; 7:56), or with understanding the import of an event (Acts 4:13; 17:22; 21:20; 27:10). That the companions do not see may imply that they are unmoved by what has occurred. Certainly they are not employed elsewhere in this account as witnesses to the reality of Saul's experience. Indeed, having made their brief appearance they vanish altogether after v. 8.

If v. 7 presents Saul's companions as unaffected by the event, vv. 8–9 convey quite the opposite regarding Saul himself. The encounter renders him helpless and Luke's repetition makes the point inescapable: Although he opens his eyes he cannot see (*blepein*, not *theōrein*). Unable to follow the command of v. 6a on his own, he must be led into Damascus by the hand. Finally, in addition to the fact that he remains blind for three days, he neither eats nor drinks.

One interpretation of vv. 8–9 understands the reference to three days to imply that Saul is undergoing death and resurrection. However, none of the other instances of that time reference in Luke lend themselves to such an interpretation (cf. Luke 2:46; Acts 25:1; 28:7, 12, 17). On the contrary, Luke, like other biblical authors, uses "three days" to refer to a short period of time, and there is no reason to see in this instance anything more.

Because Luke says that Saul did not eat or drink, other interpreters argue that this is a time of penance. Haenchen, for example, comments that the fast "demonstrates [Saul's] transformation."[18] The text does not say that this was done as penance, however, and the evidence elsewhere in Luke-Acts does not require that conclusion (cf. Luke 4:2; 7:33; Acts 23:12). In the Old Testament, various developments motivate periods of fasting. For example, Moses fasts when he is with God (Exod. 34:28); Jonathan fasts because of his anger with Saul (1 Sam. 20:34); Tobias's mother fasts because of grief (Tob. 10:7). As in those texts, the fact that Saul does not eat and drink simply reinforces the intensity and importance of what has occurred.

Verses 8–9, then, create a picture of Saul as immobilized; quite in contrast to the fiend of 9:1, he is helpless. It is reading into the text to conclude that this is death and resurrection imagery, or that Saul has undergone transformation. The state described here is neither negative nor positive. Indeed, it parallels the very first mention of Saul in 7:58, where the witnesses to Stephen's death place their cloaks at the feet of a bystander. In both places Saul is passive, and in each text Saul is introduced. That is, in addition to their function of closing off the encounter scene, vv. 8–9 also introduce the new Saul. As before, he is at first passive, and his true identity emerges only gradually.

Scene 3

> Now there was a disciple at Damascus named Ananias. The Lord said to him in a vision, "Ananias." And he said, "Here I am, Lord." And the Lord said to him, "Rise and go to the street called Straight, and inquire in the house of Judas for a man of Tarsus named Saul; for behold, he is praying, and he has seen a man named Ananias come in and lay his hands on him so that he might regain his sight." But Ananias answered, "Lord, I have heard from many about this man, how much evil he has done to thy saints at Jerusalem; and here he has authority from the chief priests to bind all who call upon thy name." But the Lord said to him, "Go, for he is a chosen instrument of mine to carry my name before the Gentiles and kings and the sons of Israel; for I will show him how much he must suffer for the sake of my name." (Acts 9:10–16)

Verse 10 clearly introduces both a new character and a new scene. Saul, who first appeared in Acts 9 over against the "disciples of the Lord," is now to be helped by one of those disciples. All that we learn about Ananias is that he is a *mathētēs* (a disciple) in Damascus. This explicit identification, not repeated in Acts 22, means that Ananias represents believers, and that is certainly the role he takes in the exchange that follows.

As is frequently the case in Acts, instructions concerning unexpected events in the mission come through visions (e.g., 10:3, 17, 19; 11:5; 16:9, 10; 18:9; cf. 2:17). When Ananias hears his name, he responds with the stereotypical formula, "Here I am" (cf. Septuagint Gen. 22:1; 1 Sam. 3:6, 8). The first stage in the instructions Ananias receives is straightforward. He is to go to a particular place and seek a particular individual. However, the *idou gar* (for behold) at the end of v. 11 announces that something surprising follows, something worthy of note (cf. Luke 1:44, 48; 2:10; 17:21).[19] In this instance two developments account for the *idou gar*: (1) Saul is praying, and (2) Saul saw Ananias come so that he might be healed.

That Saul is praying means that he has at least moved beyond the stage of immobility described in vv. 8–9. Whether his prayer implies faith is more difficult to say. Perhaps the prayer parallels Saul's earlier approval of the murder of Stephen (8:1): he consents, but he does not yet actively participate. The fact that Saul sees Ananias serves as the final part of Ananias's commission, which is not explicitly stated.

Because Ananias understands the description of Saul's vision as a commission for himself, he begins to object. What he says in vv. 13–14 recapitulates 8:3 and 9:1–2, but does so in an emphatic way. Ananias has heard about Saul "from many"; he did evil things to "your saints," and here he has authority against "all who call upon your name." In other words, Ananias says, "But this one is the enemy!"

The response of the Lord in vv. 15–16 does not acknowledge Ananias's comments or attempt to explain Saul's behavior as persecutor. Instead, it opens by repeating the simple command of v. 11, "Go." Then, like the statement of Ananias, the response centers on the identity of Saul. He is not enemy or persecutor, but "chosen instrument." In addition, like Ananias's description, the response emphasizes the relationship between Saul and the Lord: "He is *my* chosen instrument to carry *my* name . . . I will show him . . . suffer on behalf of *my* name."

In the new description of Saul, emphasis rests on the phrase *skeuos eklogēs* (chosen instrument), which stands at the beginning. In Luke, *skeuos* elsewhere appears with a literal meaning of container or vessel (Luke 8:16; 17:31; Acts 10:11, 16; 27:17). This is the only instance of the noun *eklogē* in Luke-Acts, but a related verb does occur, normally in connection with the choosing of someone for a particular role (cf. Acts 1:2, 24–25; 6:5). It is reasonable to conclude that Saul's calling is not simply that which belongs to any believer. He is chosen for a particular role.

That conclusion is reinforced by what follows. Saul is "to carry my name before the Gentiles and kings and sons of Israel." Luke nowhere else employs this exact expression (cf. Luke 14:27), but he frequently refers to the power of "the name" and belief "in the name" (e.g., Luke 24:47; Acts 2:38; 3:6; 4:10; 5:28). Indeed, one of the ironies in this scene involves the contrast between Saul as the one who persecutes those who "call on the name" (v. 14) and Saul as the one who himself bears the name (vv. 15, 16).

Saul will carry the name before "Gentiles and kings and sons of Israel." The order of these groups has caused some consternation because it does not represent the order in which Paul actually preaches. Thus, it is not obviously programmatic as is Acts 1:8, which establishes the movement of the church's preaching. Löning views this discrepancy as evidence that Luke has redacted an earlier version of the story, adding "sons of Israel" to "Gentiles and kings."[20] However, it is not necessary to posit Lukan redaction in order to account for this list, which points ahead to the time when Paul will preach before Gentiles (Acts 13:44—28:32), kings (Acts 26), and sons of Israel (Acts 22).[21] Moreover, the list moves from those who receive Paul's preaching (Gentiles) to those who hear without receiving (kings) to those who reject it (sons of Israel).

Verse 16 completes the new description of Saul by reference to the suffering that will eventually be a part of his identity. Haenchen rightly notes that the verse exactly reverses Ananias's words in vv. 13–14.[22] The one who did *hosa kaka* (how much evil) to those "who call on the name" will now suffer *hosa* "on account of my name." This verse also recalls v. 6, in which Saul hears that he will be told what it is necessary to do. Now at least part of that necessity has been revealed. He will bear the name and "it is necessary for him to suffer" *(dei pathein)*.

Scene 4

> So Ananias departed and entered the house. And laying his hands on him he said, "Brother Saul, the Lord Jesus who appeared to you on the road by which you came, has sent me that you may regain your sight and be filled with the Holy Spirit." And immediately something like scales fell from his eyes and he regained his sight. Then he rose and was baptized, and took food and was strengthened. (Acts 9:17–19a)

The beginning of scene 4 (vv. 17–19) finds Ananias fulfilling the vision of Saul exactly as v. 12 had originally described. He enters the house and lays hands upon Saul. With his first words to Saul, Ananias enacts the changed identity of Saul. He speaks no longer *about* "this man," but *to* "Saul, brother."

Ananias then explains who has sent him; it was "the Lord Jesus who appeared to you." One additional phrase refers back to Saul's encounter. The RSV translates this: "On the road by which you came." While that is an acceptable translation, it does not bring out the fact that the verb is imperfect ("on the road by which you were coming"). The continuous action of the verb, together with "way," which in v. 2 refers to believers, makes it appear that both Saul's literal road and his path of action are being referred to here. Saul saw Jesus in the middle of Saul's activity against Jesus.

Ananias's final words explain why he has come: "That you may regain your sight and be filled with the Holy Spirit." Immediately after these words, "something like scales" fell away from Saul's eyes, he regained his sight, was baptized, and was strengthened with food (vv. 18–19a).

At first glance, there seems to be some difficulty with what is said here. Ananias says that he has come so that Saul may see and receive the Spirit. In what follows, however, no mention is made of receiving the Spirit. Instead, Saul is baptized. This anomaly should not lead us to suppose that Luke believed that Saul never received the Spirit or that some earlier text has been altered. Instead, Luke describes the event by means of Ananias's words together with Saul's actions.[23]

This fourth scene bears considerable resemblance to a miracle story. The subject's illness and the intensity of the illness are not described, having already been introduced in vv. 7–9. The healing itself is tersely stated, followed by a demonstration of the cure (vv. 18–19). In the next scene, we find further evidence of the cure (v. 20) and the (delayed) amazement of the bystanders (v. 21). Unlike most healings, however, the focus here is on the subject of the healing rather than on the healer. Ananias has completely disappeared from view by the end of this scene, and Saul remains as the focus of attention.

Despite its brevity, scene 4 provides a second climactic event in the overall narrative of Acts 9. No longer reduced to inactivity or in the consensual stage of prayer, Saul here becomes active once again. He sees again, he rises to be baptized, he is strengthened by eating. The parallel to his emerging activity as persecutor in 7:58, 8:1–3, and 9:1–2 is complete.

Scene 5

For several days he was with the disciples at Damascus. And in the synagogues immediately he proclaimed Jesus, saying, "He is the Son of

God." And all who heard him were amazed, and said, "Is not this the man who made havoc in Jerusalem of those who called on this name? And he has come here for this purpose, to bring them bound before the chief priests." But Saul increased all the more in strength, and confounded the Jews who lived in Damascus by proving that Jesus was the Christ. When many days had passed, the Jews plotted to kill him, but their plot became known to Saul. They were watching the gates day and night, to kill him; but his disciples took him by night and let him down over the wall, lowering him in a basket. And when he had come to Jerusalem he attempted to join the disciples; and they were all afraid of him, for they did not believe that he was a disciple. But Barnabas took him, and brought him to the apostles, and declared to them how on the road he had seen the Lord, who spoke to him, and how at Damascus he had preached boldly in the name of Jesus. So he went in and out among them at Jerusalem, preaching boldly in the name of the Lord. And he spoke and disputed against the Hellenists; but they were seeking to kill him. And when the brethren knew it, they brought him down to Caesarea, and sent him off to Tarsus. (Acts 9:19b–30)

Scene 5 describes the result of all that has occurred and introduces certain themes that are significant throughout Luke's portrayal of Paul.[24] Crucial both for what precedes and what follows are vv. 20–21. Saul's "immediate" action is to preach that Jesus is the Son of God. As with Ananias, those who hear his preaching respond that this is the persecutor. Such a response only serves to increase the intensity of Saul's preaching (v. 22). With v. 23, the prophecy that Saul would suffer on behalf of the name begins to be fulfilled. Escaping from danger in Damascus, Saul finds that his "way" is not an easy one even in Jerusalem; they do not believe that he is a disciple (v. 26). But Barnabas defends Saul by explaining that Saul saw the Lord and that Saul preached in Jesus' name. A further conflict with the Hellenists leads to Saul's exile to Tarsus. The cycle is complete: The persecutor has become the persecuted.

What can we conclude about this narrative? Our examination demonstrates that it is primarily a story about *the reversal of an enemy*. From his very first appearance in Acts 7:58 until he departs for Tarsus in 9:30, the story centers on Saul as the enemy. He is first the active persecutor, then the immobilized persecutor, and finally the preacher whose former persecution causes suspicion. By means of the increasing activity of Saul first as persecutor and then as believer, Luke has underscored the reversal aspect of the narrative.

As a story about the overthrow of an enemy, Acts 9:1–30 fits in well with one of Luke's major themes, the power of God. Throughout his two-volume work, Luke constantly argues that God is the author of what happens. This is particularly the case when the church finds itself in adverse situations. Those who oppose the will of God find themselves thwarted.

Although this is primarily a narrative of the reversal of an enemy, it also contains a call or commissioning. The call is particularly reflected, as we have seen, in v. 6 and vv. 15–16, as well as in Saul's actions in vv. 19b–30. That is, the narrative describes Saul's call and also his initial fulfillment of that call. Because the call itself does not dominate this particular narrative, some have denied that Saul's call is even present here. They point out that the call is not given directly to Saul, but is only announced to Ananias. The call still stands in the narrative, however, and the reader, to whom the story is directed, can hardly avoid its presence. In addition, what Luke does here, consistent with his method elsewhere, is to introduce a topic that will later reappear in its developed form.[25]

At the outset of this analysis, I noted the importance of giving attention to the role played by Acts 9 in its context. Often students of Luke observe that this scene introduces Paul and provides the basis for his later work. While that is surely one function of the narrative, there are others as well. With its emphasis on Saul as an enemy of believers, who himself becomes a proclaimer of the gospel, Acts 9 is a specific and dramatic example of what is said at the beginning of Acts 8; that the adversity that befalls the church becomes opportunity for further growth and movement. As the persecution in Jerusalem forced the dispersed believers into Samaria where they preached, so also the persecutor Saul is changed into a major advocate.

Another observation about the function of Acts 9 in its context has to do with its location between the conversion of the Ethiopian eunuch and that of Cornelius. Frequently commentators note that the movement of Christian preaching outward from Jerusalem conforms to the pattern established in 1:8: "In Jerusalem and in all Judea and Samaria and to the end of the earth." With 8:4–25, the gospel moves into Samaria, and in Acts 10 we have the first official conversion of a Gentile and, hence, the gospel moves to "the end of the earth." What, however, is to be said of the conversions of the eunuch and Saul, which appear between these two events?

Answering that question will depend on our examinations of the stories of the eunuch and Cornelius in chapter 4. It is, however, appropriate to offer a few preliminary suggestions here. If Luke understands the Samaritans to be "heretical" Jews, and the eunuch to be some kind of semi-Jew, Paul as the Enemy is at the very perimeter of Judaism. Because of what he has done, he is as far from the receptive Jews in Jerusalem (Acts 2:37–42) as he can be without being a Gentile. Thus, Luke has positioned Paul's conversion in the larger narrative in such a way as to show the growing scope of the movement.

After examining the narratives in Acts 8 and 10, we shall return to these questions. These observations already suggest that the differences between Acts 9 and the other accounts of Paul's conversion need not be explained by an appeal to multiple sources or to variations of a single source. Instead the differences among the three accounts derive from the demands of diverse contexts.

ACTS 22

Luke locates the second account of Paul's conversion at a decisive point in the narrative. While resistance to Paul's preaching is a thread that runs throughout Acts, beginning even in 9:23, that thread becomes dominant when Paul announces his journey to Rome. The transition to this final stage of accusation and defense comes in 19:21: "Now after these events Paul resolved in the Spirit to pass through Macedonia and Achaia and go to Jerusalem, saying, 'After I have been there, I must also see Rome.'"

Stories that focus on conflict and statements that prophesy Paul's fate now follow each other in close succession. Immediately after Paul's announcement in 19:21 we find the riot at Ephesus, which culminates in a demand that charges be made in the courts instead of the streets (19:35–40). Brief reference to a Jewish plot against Paul occurs in 20:3. In Paul's speech to the Ephesian elders, he states that they will not see him again and hints broadly at the reason: "And now, behold, I am going to Jerusalem, bound in the Spirit, not knowing what shall befall me there; except that the Holy Spirit testifies to me in every city that imprisonment and afflictions await me" (20:22–23).

The early section of Acts 21 reinforces this sense of impending misfortune. Disciples in Tyre warn Paul through the Spirit not to go to Jerusalem (21:4). Agabus prophesies that the Jews will bind Paul and hand him over to the Gentiles (21:11). Resignation to this fate is uttered both by Paul and by his fellow believers (21:13–14).

With such an elaborate introduction, the reader is scarcely surprised when believers in Jerusalem tell Paul that he is accused of teaching against the law (21:20–21). Despite Paul's participation in the purification rite, he is seized by Jews who claim that he has both taught against the law and defiled the temple (21:27–29). In an attempt to stop the riot, a tribune arrests Paul. As he is being taken away, Paul seeks to speak to the tribune. The tribune's misunderstanding creates the situation in which Paul can identify himself and ask for permission to speak to the people.

What we call the second account of Paul's conversion, then, forms the climax to the predictions about Paul's fate in Jerusalem and introduces the series of trial scenes that culminates in Acts 26. Despite the fact that the audience is a mob, Paul offers a formal defense speech. Indeed, the speech conforms to the general pattern of defense speeches in Roman historiography. Luke has, therefore, transformed the setting so that the outdoor scene becomes a courtroom and the mob functions to some degree as judge.[26]

Verse 1 contains certain elements that are typical in introductions to defense speeches. There is a term of address to the court ("Men, brothers and fathers") as well as an acknowledgment that what follows is a defense ("hear the defense which I now make before you"). The standard praise of the court, the *captatio benevolentiae*, is missing, although v. 3 may play that role.

Verse 2 dramatically interrupts Paul with the comment that those present gave even more attention to him when they heard him speaking in "the Hebrew dialect." This comment provides a second introduction to the speech, complementary to v. 1. That is, v. 1 introduces by calling for the court's attention and announcing Paul's intent to defend himself, and v. 2 introduces by acknowledging that those present gave their full attention.

Verse 2 also further draws attention to the issue of Paul's relationship to Judaism. There have been several indications of this already. In 21:39 Paul asserts emphatically, "I am a Jew." He then asks to speak to "the people," using *laos*, the term customarily employed to refer to the Jewish people (cf. Acts 3:23; 4:8; 7:17). The final comment preceding the introduction to his speech specifies that he is speaking "in the Hebrew dialect." This comment, of course, is the basis for v. 2.

Luke has constructed the body of Paul's speech, vv. 3–21, in such a way that it defends Paul as a loyal Jew. What is said about Paul's conversion is generally consistent with Acts 9. Points at which chapter 22 and chapter 9 are inconsistent have to do almost entirely with Luke's need to portray Paul as a loyal Jew.

There are four distinct sections within the body of the speech: (1) vv. 3–5, the description of Paul's training and experience as a zealous Jew; (2) vv. 6–11, Paul's encounter with Jesus; (3) vv. 12–16, the role of Ananias; (4) vv. 17–21, Paul's vision in the temple.

Section 1

> I am a Jew, born at Tarsus in Cilicia, but brought up in this city at the feet of Gamaliel, educated according to the strict manner of the law of our fathers, being zealous for God as you all are this day. I persecuted the Way to the death, binding and delivering to prison both men and women, as the high priest and the whole council of elders bear me witness. From them I received letters to the brethren, and I journeyed to Damascus to take those also who were there and bring them in bonds to Jerusalem. (Acts 22:3–5)

Section 1 opens with another emphatic assertion of Paul's identity (cf. 21:39): "I am a Jewish man." The use of the present tense implies that this identity has not been rejected. Following this claim comes a stylized explanation of Paul's credentials that employs three perfect participles: He was "born in Tarsus of Cilicia, but was brought up in this city, educated at the feet of Gamaliel."[27] The final statement in v. 3 reverts to the present tense, "being a zealot for God just as all of you are today." Paul, like those described in 21:20, is zealous, but his zeal is "for God" by contrast with those who are zealous for the law.

In the final statement of v. 3, the goal of this first section becomes obvious. It is to establish an image of Paul as a good and loyal Jew, *in every way like his audience.* The first three verses forge a sense of identification between Paul and those who listen to him: he speaks their language, he is a Jew who was brought up in Jerusalem and educated properly, he is zealous just as they are zealous.

As Paul turns in vv. 4–5 to describe his persecution of believers, this sense of identification with his audience is maintained. There is no disjuncture between v. 3 and vv. 4–5; vv. 4–5 constitute, instead, an example of the zeal described in v. 3. The syntax itself confirms this observation, because v. 4 begins with a relative pronoun linking what follows to the antecedent "I" in v. 3: "I am a Jew . . . who persecuted." Verses 4–5 largely repeat the description of Paul's persecution in Acts 8:3 and 9:1–2. The differences that occur intensify Paul's actions and their legitimacy. In v. 4 Paul claims that he persecuted "to the death," although nothing in what follows supports that contention. What this discrepancy does, then, is to heighten the importance attached to Paul's activity by portraying it as a persecution "to death."

In v. 5 Paul invokes the chief priest and "the whole council of elders" as witnesses to his persecution. Acts 9 mentions simply that Paul sought letters from the chief priest. Here we find both the chief priest and the council. More important, they function as witnesses to Paul's persecution and, therefore, to his zeal. Haenchen's observation that the personnel would scarcely be the same after so many years only draws attention to their role in this text,[28] which is to provide further evidence of Paul's claim to be a loyal Jew.

Another slight alteration in v. 5 heightens the identification between Paul and his audience. The letters that Paul sought in Acts 9 were for "the synagogues," while 22:5 specifies that they are for "the brothers" in Damascus. It would be a mistake to overemphasize this distinction and, yet, the latter expression does connote Paul's kinship with those in Damascus in a way that the term "the synagogue" does not.

Section 2

> As I made my journey and drew near to Damascus, about noon a great light from heaven suddenly shone about me. And I fell to the ground and heard a voice saying to me, "Saul, Saul, why do you persecute me?" And I answered, "Who are you, Lord?" And he said to me, "I am Jesus of Nazareth whom you are persecuting." Now those who were with me saw the light but did not hear the voice of the one who was speaking to me. And I said, "What shall I do, Lord?" And the Lord said to me, "Rise, and go into Damascus, and there you will be told all that is appointed for

you to do." And when I could not see because of the brightness of that light, I was led by the hand of those who were with me, and came into Damascus. (Acts 22:6–11)

Up to this point in his defense, Paul heavily emphasizes his exemplary behavior and his acknowledged status among Jews in Jerusalem. With vv. 6–11, the encounter with Jesus, Paul takes up the event which reversed his attitude to the "Way." This section parallels 9:3–9, and the similarities are extensive. There are more verbal parallels here than elsewhere in the two accounts. Nevertheless, the differences that do occur are important.

Perhaps the most striking differences pertain to the presence of the light. Verse 6 specifies that the light appeared "about noon." Since noon is the very time when natural light would have been at its peak, the implication is that this is a brilliant light indeed. Luke also notes that it was a great or large light, an intensifying adjective not present in the first account. At the end of the section, v. 11 explains that Paul could not see "because of the brightness of that light," again emphasizing its power and import. This emphasis underscores the reality and significance of Paul's experience.

Paul refers to the light one other time when in v. 9 he says that his companions saw the light. Students of Acts have long worried about the conflict between this verse and 9:7:

Now those who were with me saw the light but did not hear the voice of the one who was speaking to me. (22:9)

The men who were traveling with him stood speechless, hearing the voice but seeing no one. (9:7)

Among the solutions offered for this problem are source theories, attempts to distinguish the hearing of 9:7 from that of 22:9, and suggestions that in Acts 22 Luke is correcting his source in chapter 9. However, if we give adequate attention to the function of this verse in the story, the differences cease to have much weight.

To begin with, it should be noted that 22:9 appears at a different point in the account than does 9:7. In the first account of Paul's conversion, the companions' response is mentioned only after the dialogue between Jesus and Paul. Their response contrasts with that of Paul in that they do not perceive what has occurred. The second account, on the other hand, inserts the response of the companions within the dialogue of Jesus and Paul.

Standing in the middle of the dialogue as it does, the comment about the companions has two functions. It once again calls attention to the light, thereby verifying Paul's claims about the light and the experience because others saw the light as well. It also heightens the drama of the encounter by emphasizing that only Paul heard what was said. Although the encounter had a character that all could see, only Paul heard what was said, especially the words that point forward to his particular commission. This explanation of the function of 22:9 in its context does not eliminate the contradictions between 22:9 and 9:7. It suggests, instead, that Luke has two somewhat different points to make with the same story and that the minor contradictions that arise are a result of those different points.

In addition to differences having to do with the light and the companions, the second account of Paul's encounter with Jesus presents a slightly altered understanding of Paul's response to the event. Here Paul remains an active participant, never quite as incapacitated as 9:8–9 would suggest. In Acts 9, Paul's only words at the encounter are, "Who are you, sir?" Here he takes the initiative to ask at least, "What should I do, sir?" Although in v. 11 Paul concedes that he could not see and was led by the hand, he still says, "I went into Damascus." The first account, on the other hand, specifies that Paul's companions took him by the hand and led him into Damascus (9:8). There is also in Acts 22 no reference to a period of fasting. Thus, at the close of section 2, Paul is left waiting for the fulfillment of Jesus' words in v. 10.

Before taking up section 3, two other features of this encounter need to be noted. Jesus' words in 22:8 repeat those in 9:5 almost exactly. The single difference is that in 22:8 Jesus adds the qualification, "the Nazarene." This noun occurs eight times in Luke-Acts, always in the context of a Jewish audience.[29] Its appearance here further indicates that Luke has shaped this account of Paul's conversion to its setting in the defense of Paul in Jerusalem.

The second feature that requires attention is found in v. 10b. There Jesus announces to Paul that in Damascus "it will be told you concerning all of the things that it has been ordered for you to do" (au. trans.). Although 9:6 indicates the necessity of Paul's work, this statement is less ambiguous and more emphatic. "All the things" makes it clear that this is not simply a reference to baptism, but an announcement about a commission.

Section 3

> And one Ananias, a devout man according to the law, well spoken of by all the Jews who lived there, came to me, and standing by me said to me, "Brother Saul, receive your sight." And in that very hour I received my sight and saw him. And he said, "The God of our fathers appointed you to know his will, to see the Just One and to hear a voice from his mouth; for you will be a witness for him to all men of what you have seen and heard. And now why do you wait? Rise and be baptized, and wash away your sins, calling on his name." (Acts 22:12–16)

That commission becomes more prominent in the third section of Paul's speech, the visit of Ananias (vv. 12–16). Unlike Acts 9, Luke includes in the speech no description of Ananias's vision or Ananias's objections regarding Paul. While some suggest that the two accounts differ because Paul did not know Ananias's experience or because Luke employs a different source here, the variation probably depends again on Luke's goal in this scene. One concern in Acts 9 is to show that believers had to be persuaded that Paul had actually ceased to be their enemy. That issue is altogether missing in the second account; thus, Ananias's conversation with the Lord drops out as well.

Indeed, Acts 22 does not explicitly say that Ananias is a believer, in contrast to the term "disciple" in 9:10. Ananias instead is described as "a man pious with respect to the law, as witnessed by all the Jewish inhabitants" (au. trans.). He is, first of all, "pious," an adjective with which Luke characterizes Simeon (Luke 2:25), the Jews present at Pentecost (Acts 2:5), and those who mourned the death of Stephen (Acts 8:2). That Ananias is described as being pious "according to the law" further enhances his credibility with Paul's audience. The final element in Ananias's description also appeals to that credibility. Ananias's faithfulness is witnessed by "all the Jews" in Damascus. Just as Paul earlier appealed to the high priest and the council as witnesses for himself, so now he appeals to the Jews as witnesses for Ananias. Haenchen comments that Ananias is, in Acts 22, not a disciple but "only" a devout Jew of good reputation.[30] That comparison misses the point that Luke is making, which is that a faithful Jew of unquestionable reputation came to Paul and relayed Paul's calling.

Apart from the greeting, "Saul, brother," Ananias's words to Paul in Acts 22 bear little resemblance to the words in chapter 9. In 9:17, Ananias simply claims that he has been sent by the Lord in order that Paul might receive both his sight and the Spirit. Acts 22, on the other hand, deals with the restoration of Paul's sight in a very cursory fashion in order to concentrate on Paul's calling.

Verse 14 emphasizes the fact of Paul's calling, its origin in God. "The God of our fathers" is a traditional way of referring to the God of Israel (e.g., Gen. 43:23; 46:1; Exod. 3:13; Deut. 1:11; Josh. 1:11; 1 Chron. 5:25; 12:17) by contrast with "Jesus who appeared to you" in 9:17. It is the God of Israel's past who chose Paul, and that choice is amplified in three ways: "To know his will, to see the Just One, and to hear his voice."

Ananias's statement reaches its main point in v. 15. God chose Paul so that he would be a "witness for him to all persons of the things you have seen and heard." The term "witness" links Paul with the mission given to the apostles in 1:8 and with their activity throughout Acts (e.g., 1:22; 2:32; 3:15; 5:32; 10:39; 13:31).[31] At this point Paul's witness is described as a witness *pros pantas anthrōpous* (to all persons). While that certainly includes Gentiles, they are not explicitly named just yet. Paul is to witness to "the things you saw and heard." Surely this refers not simply to the encounter with Jesus, but to all that has occurred to Paul up until this point in Acts. The comment recalls for the reader all of Paul's experiences.

In v. 16 the role of Ananias comes to an end. He concludes his description of Paul's commission by telling Paul to rise, be baptized, and wash away his sins. The brevity of this command suggests that Luke has little interest in this part of the meeting between Paul and Ananias. He relies on stereotypical expressions which he uses without further explanation.

What Luke has done in this section of Paul's speech is once again to place Paul's experience in a context that would be understood by a Jewish audience. He first heard that he was to be a witness from Ananias, a pious Jew acceptable to the whole Jewish community. Ananias described the one who called Paul as the God of Israel, never mentioning the name of Jesus. In other words, everything in this section seeks to maintain the identification between Paul and his hearers that was established back in v. 3.

Scene 4

> When I had returned to Jerusalem and was praying in the temple, I fell into a trance and saw him saying to me, "Make haste and get quickly out of Jerusalem, because they will not accept your testimony about me." And I said, "Lord, they themselves know that in every synagogue I imprisoned and beat those who believed in thee. And when the blood of Stephen thy witness was shed, I also was standing by and approving, and keeping the garments of those who killed him." And he said to me, "Depart; for I will send you far away to the Gentiles." (Acts 22:17–21)

Although the final section (vv. 17–21) affirms once again Paul's loyalty to Judaism, it also presents the reason for the final break between Paul and his audience. Perhaps because Paul's vision in the temple is unique to this account, commentators sometimes treat it as an appendix to the conversion event, something not integral to the story itself. However, the connections between vv. 17–21 and the rest of Paul's speech are such that the temple scene must be viewed not simply as a part of the speech, but *as its climax.*

The first connection between vv. 17–21 and what precedes has to do with the context. The final stage in Paul's "call" occurs in Jerusalem, where he began his persecution (vv. 4–5), and where he now defends himself. Paul is not only in Jerusalem when he has his vision, but he is in the temple praying. Surely someone who has come to the temple to pray is to be recognized as a faithful Jew.

What follows in the dialogue of vv. 18–21 is, at first glance, perplexing. Paul hears the command: "Hasten and go out quickly from Jerusalem, because they will not receive your witness about me." For the first time in the speech, the tension between Paul's message and the Jews is mentioned. Until this point, the speech assumes their agreement.

Paul's response in vv. 19–20 does not directly address this claim about the Jews of Jerusalem. It also neither consents to the order to flee nor refuses that order. Instead, Paul appeals to his past and to the Jewish understanding of that past:

> Lord, they understand that I was imprisoning and beating throughout the synagogues those who believe in you. And when the blood of Stephen your witness was poured out, I myself was present and consenting and protecting the cloaks of those who killed him. (au. trans.)

What is the connection between this bit of information and the command that precedes it? Paul claims that the Jerusalem Jews know what he once did against the church. The unstated connection is that they should accept his witness *because* they know his past. Since they know what he once did, they should listen as he explains why he now preaches Jesus as the Christ.

Verse 21 does not reject Paul's claim but ignores it and moves on to the final expression of Paul's calling: "Depart, because I will send you far away to the Gentiles." Here the specific nature of Paul's witness is named for the first time. He is to go to the Gentiles. Not surprisingly, here also the speech breaks off or, rather, it is interrupted by the audience. Luke explains that they listened "up to this word" and then cried out: "Away with such a fellow from the earth! For he ought not to live." The main point of Paul's speech has been reached, and that very point has been rejected by the audience.[32]

While we pull together what we have learned about this text, we want to keep in mind both its variations from Acts 9 and its function in the present context. As was the case with the first account, Luke has shaped the account to the demands of the defense speech and its context. By contrast with Acts 9, Paul's first defense speech begins with an extensive assertion of Paul's place among loyal and faithful Jews. The description of his encounter with Jesus emphasizes the reality of the light that accompanied the event, and says little about Paul's immobility following it. Ananias is, in this instance, not a representative believer but a devout Jew of good repute who mediates Paul's calling. Finally, Luke introduces the temple scene in which Paul's particular call is announced directly by God. The speech provides a dramatic opening for Paul's defense. Charges that Paul teaches against the law and defiles the temple are not explicitly countered, and yet the whole speech rejects them by means of its portrayal of Paul as "zealous for God" and as moved directly by God.

What we find in Acts 22 is not a different source or a corrected source. It is the same story that appeared in Acts 9, but altered in such a way as to make the points Luke needs to make here. Instead of the "overthrow of the enemy," we have in Acts 22 "the call of the faithful Jew." Where the calling of Paul was introduced in chapter 9 but not developed, in chapter 22 it swallows up the story. Jesus tells Paul that he will have a calling, Ananias announces that it is from God, and the temple scene confirms and specifies it. The divine calling constitutes Paul's defense and the nature of that calling leads to Paul's rejection in Jerusalem. We turn now to Acts 26, in order to ask what becomes of the conversion in its third setting.

ACTS 26

Luke's narrative of Paul's trials and defense culminates in Acts 26, which includes the third account of Paul's conversion. As we have already seen, the early charges against Paul in Jerusalem are that he teaches against the law and the people, and that he defiled the temple (21:21, 28). Paul responds to these charges in Acts 22 by arguing that he too is zealous for God and has done only what he had been directed to do. The intervening chapters describe additional charges against Paul: He is a "pestilent fellow, an agitator among all the Jews throughout the world, and a ringleader among the sect of the Nazarenes . . . [who] tried to profane the temple" (24:5–6). Paul argues, in his defense, that he has always maintained Jewish tradition and has caused no troubles (24:11–13; 25:10); moreover, Paul claims that he is actually accused because he believes in the resurrection (23:6; 24:21). Twice Luke includes accounts of plots to kill Paul (23:12–15; 25:2–5). When Festus eventually offers to send Paul to Jerusalem for trial, Paul instead appeals to Caesar (25:11).

Following this appeal, Agrippa and Bernice arrive in Caesarea. Festus explains Paul's situation to them and acknowledges that the Jews have no real charges against him (25:13–21). When Agrippa agrees to hear Paul himself, Festus introduces Paul as "the man about whom the whole Jewish people petitioned me." He again acknowledges that Paul has done nothing deserving of death. Admitting that he has no charges to send to Caesar regarding Paul (25:23–27), Festus hopes that Agrippa will help him formulate the accusations.

With Festus's repeated statements that there are no real charges against Paul, Luke proclaims Paul innocent even prior to the defense speech. Paul responds here not to specific charges brought before Festus and Agrippa, but to all the accusations that have been made against him. The third account of Paul's conversion thus has climactic significance.[33]

> Agrippa said to Paul, "You have permission to speak for yourself." Then Paul stretched out his hand and made his defense: "I think myself fortunate that it is before you, King Agrippa, I am to make my defense

today against all the accusations of the Jews, because you are especially familiar with all customs and controversies of the Jews; therefore I beg you to listen to me patiently. My manner of life from my youth, spent from the beginning among my own nation and at Jerusalem, is known by all the Jews. They have known for a long time, if they are willing to testify, that according to the strictest party of our religion I have lived as a Pharisee." (Acts 26:1–5)

In 26:1, Agrippa grants Paul permission to speak. Luke describes Paul as stretching out his hand in the traditional pose of the orator, and Luke explicitly says that Paul was defending himself. The RSV translates the imperfect verb as "[he] made his defense," but it might well be translated, "he kept defending himself." This possibility suggests that Luke understands what follows to be the continuation of Paul's defense, rather than the beginning of a new defense.[34]

Verses 2–3 contain elements of a classic introduction to a defense speech. Paul uses a term of direct address, "King Agrippa," which will be repeated in v. 19. He explicitly states that he is about to defend himself, reinforcing v. 1. He also includes the *captatio benevolentiae* (vv. 2–3), praise of the judge which is designed to win the judge's favor: Paul is fortunate to defend himself before one who knows all the customs and debates of the Jews.

Within the *captatio benevolentiae*, Paul refers to the fact that he is accused. This technical reference to legal accusation against someone occurs at two other points in Acts. When Demetrius and his colleagues riot because of the threat posed to their livelihood by Christians, they are urged to bring charges through the legal system rather than to create a civil disturbance (19:38). Again, in Acts 23, Claudius Lysias writes to Felix that Paul has been accused (23:28) only regarding certain Jewish debates (cf. 26:3). The reappearance of this technical term for accusation in 26:2 provides a further link between this final defense and the other procedures against Paul.

Paul credits Agrippa with knowing "all customs and controversies of the Jews." This remark has occasioned considerable speculation about Agrippa, and particularly about whether Luke regarded Agrippa as a Jew. What that speculation often overlooks, however, is how the comment functions in its context. Paul is about to present a defense of himself as the victim of an intramural quarrel regarding resurrection from the dead, and thus the appeal to Agrippa's knowledge serves to introduce the lines of Paul's defense. This is not a matter of charges deserving death, but of "customs and controversies."

Before taking up the defense itself, it will be helpful to compare this introduction with the introduction to Paul's speech in Acts 22. As we have seen, both contain certain elements characteristic of defense speeches (the direct address to the audience and the explicit claim to be offering an apology). However, even in the introductions it is clear that the differences between the audiences have shaped the speeches. In 22:1–2, Paul addresses his "brothers and fathers" in Hebrew. The speech in Acts 26, by contrast, refers to the customs and controversies "of the Jews," as if Paul were somehow distinct from that group. Throughout the speech in Acts 26 Paul will claim not that he is a loyal and zealous Jew (22:3), but simply that he stands within the limits of Judaism and that he is accused because he believes in the resurrection.

Paul begins the body of his speech by reference to his past: "My manner of life from my youth. . . ." Paul does not yet explain what his "manner of life" was. Instead, he refers to time and place ("spent from the beginning among my own nation and at Jerusalem"). He also claims that *all* Jews know about him and can testify about him. At last he describes his "manner of life": I lived as a Pharisee.

The description of the Pharisaic life in v. 5 again demonstrates that this speech has been shaped by its context. In contrast to 22:3, where Paul identifies himself with his Jewish brethren, here he employs terms that are slightly more distant and objective. He categorizes the Pharisees as a party or sect, using a term that is descriptive, one that an outsider would use (cf. Acts 5:17; 15:5; 24:5, 14; 28:22). Similarly, "religion" *(thrēskeia)* refers to cult or ritual, sometimes in a highly pejorative manner (e.g., Col. 2:18; Wisd. of Sol. 14:18, 27; Philo, *On the Special Laws* 1.315). I am not suggesting that Paul's speech denigrates his past by the use of these terms, but that the terms describe his experience to a knowledgeable but *uninvolved* observer, Agrippa.

Verse 5 marks the first time Paul is characterized as a Pharisee in the conversion narratives. Indeed, only one other time in Acts do we find Paul explicitly identified as a Pharisee. That is in his defense in Acts 23, where he succeeds in dividing the audience by appealing to his Pharisaic belief in the resurrection of the dead (23:6–10).

With the "and now" of v. 6, Paul turns from the past to which "all Jews" could testify and addresses his present situation. As is the case elsewhere in Acts, the phrase "and now" announces new material or the new consequences of something that has already occurred (cf. Acts 3:17; 5:38; 20:22; 20:25). Here it marks the transition to the new situation that has separated Paul from the "manner of life" referred to in v. 4.

Verses 6–23 form a chiasm, an inverse parallelism. Paul at first claims that he is accused because of his hope, which is simply the hope of the forebears (vv. 6–8). Then he describes his persecution of Christians (vv. 9–11). Verses 12–18 concern his encounter with Jesus, which here becomes a commission. In vv. 19–20 this commission is restated, as Paul notes his obedience to it. The topic of persecution is repeated in v. 21, although here it is Paul's persecution by Jews. Finally, vv. 22–23 restate Paul's opening claim that his belief in the resurrection is consistent with the prophets and Moses. The resultant chiasm can be illustrated as follows:

1. Paul conforms to tradition in his belief in resurrection (vv. 6–8).
2. He persecuted Christians (vv. 9–11).
3. He received a call (vv. 12–18).

6. Paul conforms to tradition (vv. 22–23).
5. He has been persecuted (v. 21).
4. He obeyed his call (vv. 19–20).

Section 1

And now I stand here on trial for hope in the promise made by God to our fathers, to which our twelve tribes hope to attain, as they earnestly worship night and day. And for this hope I am accused by Jews, O king! Why is it thought incredible by any of you that God raises the dead? (Acts 26:6–8)

The first section of the chiasm repeats aspects of Paul's earlier defense. In 23:6 he successfully divides his opponents by charging that he is accused concerning "hope and the resurrection of the dead." Before Felix, in Acts 24, Paul confesses that he serves God and has hope that there will be resurrection. But vv. 6–8 do not merely repeat Paul's earlier defense; they echo concerns that appear throughout Luke-Acts. Paul's description of the twelve tribes that served in hope is reminiscent of Anna, who served "night and day" (Luke

2:37). The promise, which here appears to be promise of the resurrection (cf. Acts 13:32), Luke earlier connects with the gift of the Holy Spirit (Luke 24:49; Acts 1:4; 2:33) and with the coming of Jesus as the Messiah (Acts 2:39; 13:23).

Since Paul's belief in the resurrection of Jesus does not figure in either of the earlier conversion accounts, Frederick Veltmann argues that the conversion is narrated again because it is in his conversion that Paul came to know the truth about the resurrection.[35] However, the speech does not connect the two in any explicit way. Moreover, the statement about the resurrection in v. 8 is followed immediately by the description of Paul's persecution, not by the encounter with Jesus.

Section 2

> I myself was convinced that I ought to do many things in opposing the name of Jesus of Nazareth. And I did so in Jerusalem; I not only shut up many of the saints in prison, by authority from the chief priests, but when they were put to death I cast my vote against them. And I punished them often in all the synagogues and tried to make them blaspheme; and in raging fury against them, I persecuted them even to foreign cities. (Acts 26:9–11)

These verses present the most elaborate of Luke's descriptions of Paul's activity as persecutor. Here the elements of his persecution as described in Acts 9 and 22 are repeated and expanded. He introduces this endeavor with the only explanation given for it ("I thought it necessary to do many things against the name of Jesus of Nazareth" [au. trans.]), although he still gives no indication as to his motivation.

Instead of describing Paul as "breathing threat and murder" or persecuting the way "to death," the third account lists his deeds. First, he operated in Jerusalem (v. 10), where he not only locked up believers (cf. 8:3; 22:4) but voted against them when they were executed. Then, in all the synagogues, he punished believers and compelled them to blaspheme (v. 11a). Finally, because he was enraged with them, he pursued them "even into the outer cities."

This third account elaborates on what has already been said in Acts 9 and 22. As Haenchen notes, without this intensification "the speech would be an anti-climax in comparison with the earlier ones."[36] This version of the persecution also demonstrates Paul's statement that he "thought it necessary to do many things against the name of Jesus of

Nazareth," in distinction from chapter 22, where his persecution demonstrates his zeal.

Section 3

> Thus I journeyed to Damascus with the authority and commission of the chief priests. At midday, O king, I saw on the way a light from heaven, brighter than the sun, shining round me and those who journeyed with me. And when we had all fallen to the ground, I heard a voice saying to me in the Hebrew language, "Saul, Saul, why do you persecute me? It hurts you to kick against the goads." And I said, "Who are you, Lord?" And the Lord said, "I am Jesus whom you are persecuting. But rise and stand upon your feet; for I have appeared to you for this purpose, to appoint you to serve and bear witness to the things in which you have seen me and to those in which I will appear to you, delivering you from the people and from the Gentiles—to whom I send you to open their eyes, that they may turn from darkness to light and from the power of Satan to God, that they may receive forgiveness of sins and a place among those who are sanctified by faith in me. (Acts 26:12–18)

With v. 12, Paul's defense turns to his encounter with Jesus. As in the earlier versions, that encounter occurs while he is going to Damascus. Paul once again asserts that he traveled with the permission of the high priests. This time he does not specify what his task in Damascus was to be (cf. 9:2; 22:5), although v. 11 surely makes that clear. In Acts 26, Paul's persecution is so extensive and intensive that the trip to Damascus is only one example of persecution in the "outer cities." The encounter itself differs substantially from earlier accounts. No mention is made here of Paul's blindness as a result of the experience (cf. 9:8; 22:11). There is also no reference to Ananias. In general, as we shall see, this narrative of the encounter moves quickly over its initial aspects and concentrates on Paul's call (vv. 16b–18).

Verse 13 opens the encounter in a way that closely parallels 9:3b and 22:6. At the middle of the day Paul sees a heavenly light. Here the phrase "brighter than the sun" makes explicit the significance of the element of time; that is, the light was strong enough to be impressive even in the midday sun. This light shone around *Paul and his companions,* and they all fell to the ground (v. 14a). Unlike the previous accounts, this one does not require that someone lead Paul into Damascus; hence, the role of the companions is reduced to their mere presence in vv. 13b and 14a.

When all had fallen to the ground, Paul heard a voice "in the

Hebrew language." Jesus' first words to Paul are exactly those of 9:4 and 22:7: "Saul, Saul, why do you persecute me?" What follows that initial question does not appear in the earlier accounts: "It is hard for you to kick against the goads" (26:14, au. trans.). Despite the fact that Paul has said Jesus addressed him in Hebrew, this expression occurs only in Greek sources, where it commonly refers to the futility of resisting a greater power.[37] In this context the saying interprets the question preceding it. For Paul to persecute Jesus is to "kick against the goads," or to resist an irresistible power. The saying thus characterizes Paul's persecution. Because it is a Greek proverb, it also provides another indication that this final version of the conversion has been adapted for the scene. The saying would have had little meaning in Acts 22.

Verse 15 is almost identical to 9:5 and 22:8. Luke does not repeat the description of Jesus as "the Nazarene," which we find in 22:8 before a Jewish audience. The other slight change is that Jesus' response to Paul's question, "Who are you, sir?" is introduced by "the *kyrios* said" rather than "he said." In the first account Paul only acknowledges Jesus as Lord when Paul proclaims that publicly in 9:20. Here, however, there is less interest in sustaining the drama of the encounter than in moving quickly to the *result* of that encounter.

That result emerges in vv. 16–18, when Jesus himself announces to Paul the nature of Paul's work. Jesus commands, "Rise and stand on your feet." Jesus does not even mention a trip into Damascus (cf. 9:6; 22:10). Instead he moves directly to Paul's call and underscores the importance of what he is about to tell Paul by saying, "For this reason I appeared to you . . ." The phrase "I appeared" (*ōphthēn*) is almost a technical term for an experience of revelation (e.g., Luke 1:11; 22:43; Acts 7:2, 30). Certainly Luke understands the earlier accounts of Paul's conversion as revelatory (e.g., 9:17), but this is the only one in which Jesus *announces* that he is revealing himself.

Jesus appears in order "to appoint you servant and witness both of the things which you saw me and which I shall reveal to you, delivering you from the people and from the Gentiles, to whom I send you . . ." (vv. 16b–17, au. trans.). A first glance at this text raises several questions. How can Paul witness to things he has already seen if this is his first revelation of Jesus? In what sense is Jesus "delivering" Paul from the people and the Gentiles? Addressing these difficulties can produce exegetical contortions, unless it is recognized that Luke has placed this statement of Paul's commission in two settings. It is, of course, located in a narrative of Paul's conversion and, as such, it describes the beginning of Paul's witness and mission. However, this commission also stands in Paul's final defense speech, at the climax of Luke's defense of Paul, where it summarizes Paul's work. For that reason, the commission refers to "things you *saw*" and the rescue of Paul. Both the situation of the conversion and the work Paul has done are reflected in the commission.

First Paul learns that he has been appointed "servant and witness." The reference to servant *(hypēretēs)* recalls the prologue to Luke's Gospel, in which he speaks of the "servants of the word." K. H. Rengstorf has rightly noted that the *kai* (and) that appears in "servant and witness" is epexegetical, that is, Paul's servanthood is described by the term "witness." "Servant," then, is the term that dominates all of Acts 26:16–18; the text emphasizes Paul's task, not his possession of revelatory experience or his prerogatives.[38]

Luke employs the term "witness" to describe the work of the apostles. Prior to his ascension Jesus tells them that they will be witnesses (Luke 24:48; Acts 1:8), and Luke regularly characterizes them as such (Acts 1:22; 2:32; 3:15; 5:32; 10:39, 41; 13:31). For Paul to be called a witness (cf. 22:15) is for his work to be considered the same as that of the Twelve, even though he cannot properly be called an apostle.

Paul is to be a witness "to the things in which you have seen me and to those in which I will appear to you." Probably the personal pronoun "me" did not appear in the original and represents a later scribe's clarification of the text.[39] If we omit the pronoun, the compound clause that remains reads "the things which you saw and which I will be seen by you" (au. trans.). The awkwardness of this last clause has led to the suggestion that the order of the text is corrupt, but that conclusion is unwarranted. In order to parallel the second clause with the first, Luke has tolerated this awkward wording. The two clauses together refer to what Paul has seen by way of revelation. As noted above, the fact that the text refers to things Paul *has already* seen does not constitute a real difficulty if we bear in mind that this scene is also Luke's final defense of Paul and, as such, refers to all that has happened to him.

Verse 17 similarly refers to the experience of Paul and to his task: "Delivering you from the people and from the Gentiles—to whom I send you." Because at the time of his conversion Paul had not been in need of rescue, some have argued that the Greek should be translated "choosing" instead of "delivering." While *exairein* can be translated in that way, it never has that connotation in Acts (7:10, 34; 12:11; 23:27; cf. Jer. 1:7–8). Surely Luke understood these words to be a description of what had continually occurred: Paul, like other leaders of the church, was delivered from danger.

Paul is delivered from "the people" (i.e., the Jews) and from the Gentiles, to whom he is sent. Although the developing narrative of Acts inclines us to think that the "whom" refers to the Gentiles, nothing in the verse allows us to distinguish between the two. Indeed, instead of being preoccupied with that issue, we need to notice that v. 17 again characterizes Paul's experience as a call to service: "To whom I send you."

In our study of the account of Paul's conversion in Acts 22, we saw that the narrative culminates in the temple scene, where Paul learns that he is to go to the Gentiles. Here the statement that he is being sent is elaborated in v. 18 by means of stereotypical conversion language.

Paul is first told that he is "to open their eyes." Imagery about blindness and the giving of sight appears frequently in Luke-Acts (Luke 2:30; 4:18; 24:16, 31; Acts 9:8, 18, 40; 13:11; 28:27). Here Luke is surely dependent on Isa. 42:6–7, "I have given you as a covenant to the people, a light to the nations, to open the eyes that are blind." This description of Paul's work complements the language of v. 16. There Jesus announces that he has appeared to Paul (literally, "I was seen") and refers to what Paul has seen and will see. Here, his own task is to open the eyes of others, in order that they also may see.[40]

With the next infinitive phrase, we encounter an ambiguity that complicates translation. "To turn from darkness to light and from the authority of Satan to God" may have as its subject either the "you" of v. 17 or the "they" that appears later in v. 18. Thus, the KJV reads:

> I send *thee to open their eyes, and to turn them* from darkness to light, and from the power of Satan to God.

The RSV, on the other hand, reads as follows:

> I send *you to open their eyes, that they may turn* from darkness to light and from the power of Satan to God.

Grammatical considerations alone will not resolve this ambiguity; what follows in v. 20 suggests that it is the ones who hear Paul who themselves turn ("I declared . . . that they should repent and turn to God"). This is consistent with the use of *epistrephein* elsewhere in Acts.[41]

> Repent, therefore, and turn again, that your sins may be blotted out . . . (3:19)

> And all the residents of Lydda and Sharon saw him, and they turned to the Lord. (9:35)

> And the hand of the Lord was with them, and a great number that believed turned to the Lord. (11:21)

> You should turn from these vain things to a living God who made the heaven and the earth and the sea and all that is in them. (14:15)

> Therefore my judgment is that we should not trouble those of the Gentiles who turn to God . . . (15:19)

In Acts, those who respond positively to Christian preaching do so by "turning" to God. It seems probable, then, that "to turn from darkness to light" refers to the action of those who hear rather than to Paul's action.

The phrase "from darkness to light" is usually regarded as an allusion to Isa. 42:16, "I will turn the darkness before them into light." However, imagery regarding light and darkness is standard in descriptions of conversion:

> But you are a chosen race, a royal priesthood, a holy nation, God's own people, that you may declare the wonderful deeds of him who called you out of darkness into the marvelous light. (1 Pet. 2:9)

> They [proselytes] have shown the godliness of heart all leads to friendship and affinity, and we must rejoice with them, as if, though blind at the first they had recovered their sight and had come from the deepest darkness to behold the most radiant light. (Philo, *On Virtue* 179)

> The one who made all things alive, and called from darkness into the light, and from error into truth, and from death to life. (*Joseph and Asenath* 8.10)

> Blessed is the Lord God, who sent you to deliver me from darkness and to lead me up into the light. (*Joseph and Asenath* 15.13)

And I said, Blessed, O Lord, are they
who are planted in Thy land
And who have a place in Thy Paradise;
And who grow in the growth of Thy trees,
and have passed from darkness into light.
(*Odes of Solomon* 14.18–19)

Thus, Luke may be drawing on stereotypical conversion language as much as he is on Isaiah.

Luke underscores this stark contrast in the next phrase: "From darkness to light and from the power of Satan to God." Although Luke elsewhere describes believers as "turning to God," this is the only instance in which he further describes them as turning from Satan. The notion that conversion involves a move from Satan or from powers of evil, however, is found elsewhere in the New Testament (Eph. 2:2; Col. 1:13).

The conclusion of v. 18 takes up the consequences of turning to God: "That they may receive forgiveness of sins and a place among those who are sanctified by faith in me." Forgiveness of sins is a typically Lukan concern, appearing in the preaching of John the Baptist (Luke 1:77; 3:3) and in that of Jesus (Luke 4:18). In the church's preaching, forgiveness of sins appears as one of God's central gifts through the coming of Jesus (Acts 2:38; 5:31; 10:43; 13:38). To receive "a place among those who are sanctified" is to receive the positive gift of a share in the community (cf. Acts 20:32; Deut. 33:3; Wisd. of Sol. 5:5).

With these words Paul's description of his encounter with Jesus comes to an end. This description differs a great deal from those found in Acts 9 and 22. Here the work Paul is to do becomes the major point of the encounter. The light that overcomes Paul (v. 13) and the things he sees (v. 16) become the light to which his hearers turn when their eyes are opened (v. 18). Jesus appears *in order* to choose Paul as a servant who witnesses.

Section 4

Wherefore, O King Agrippa, I was not disobedient to the heavenly vision, but declared first to those at Damascus, then at Jerusalem and throughout all the country of Judea, and also to the Gentiles, that they should repent and turn to God and perform deeds worthy of their repentance. (Acts 26:19–20)

This elaborate statement of Paul's commission forms the center of the chiasm noted above. With v. 19 the restatement of the earlier themes begins as Paul asserts his obedience to the commission: "Wherefore, O King Agrippa, I was not disobedient to the heavenly vision, but declared first to those at Damascus, then at Jerusalem and throughout all the country of Judea, and also to the Gentiles, that they should repent and turn to God and perform deeds worthy of their repentance." The *litotes* (i.e., stylized understatement) with which this claim begins underscores all that follows: "I was obedient!" Although the sequence of places in which Paul preached does not slavishly repeat Luke's narrative, it does reflect the promise of Jesus in Acts 1:8. Paul has not only obeyed the "heavenly vision"; he has also fulfilled the promise of the Risen Lord to the apostles.

Paul's terse summary of his preaching largely recapitulates vv. 17–18. He urged that they should repent and turn to God and perform deeds worthy of their repentance. Although a distinction is often drawn between "to repent" *(metanoun)* and "to convert" *(epistrephein)* in Luke as elsewhere, the two terms are virtually interchangeable (see Acts 20:21). The presence of both here simply intensifies what Paul says regarding his preaching.

The admonition to do "deeds worthy of their repentance" introduces a topic not explicit in vv. 17–18. Repentance and turning are to be accompanied by deeds of repentance. The wording of this claim is reminiscent of Luke 3:8, in which John the Baptist addresses those who come to be baptized, "Bear fruits that befit repentance." We do not find the same formulation of this demand elsewhere in Acts; nevertheless, Luke does describe actions that illustrate repentance just following incidents of conversion (e.g., Acts 2:41–47; 4:4, 32–37). Thus, the admonition may simply make explicit what is assumed throughout the narrative.

Section 5

For this reason the Jews seized me in the temple and tried to kill me. (Acts 26:21)

Verse 21 describes the reaction to Paul's preaching: "For this reason the Jews seized me in the temple and tried to kill me." The "seizing" of Paul echoes that of Jesus (Acts 1:16) and Peter (12:3). It also reverses the earlier persecution in which Paul participated; one who earlier voted for the death of believers (26:10) now becomes the object of similar action.

Section 6

> To this day I have had the help that comes from God, and so I stand here testifying both to small and great, saying nothing but what the prophets and Moses said would come to pass: that the Christ must suffer, and that, by being the first to rise from the dead, he would proclaim light both to the people and to the Gentiles. (Acts 26:22–23)

In vv. 22–23 the defense of Paul concludes with his assertion that he has always had God's help as he witnesses to all people. His witness differs not from what was said by the prophets and Moses; that is, that Christ would suffer and would rise from the dead to proclaim light to the people and the Gentiles. This conclusion takes up Paul's opening remarks and thus completes the chiasm: Paul is innocent because he preaches only what has always been expected by Israel.

Festus's reaction to Paul's defense marks the conclusion of the speech. The closing dialogue between Paul and his audience allows him to assert emphatically the truth of what he says (vv. 24–29). Agrippa and Festus pronounce the final judgment: "This man is doing nothing to deserve death or imprisonment." The trial that was intended to provide them with charges to send to Rome against Paul has instead resulted in his acquittal. Paul will go to Rome, but only because he himself had appealed to Caesar.

What can we conclude from this study of Luke's third narration of the conversion of Paul? Because of its setting within a defense speech, this account invites comparison with that in Acts 22. Yet the audiences for the two speeches differ and those differences account for some details in the narrative. Here Paul addresses not the "brothers" but the representatives of the Roman Empire. He speaks of the "customs" and "debates" of a "religion," not of "zeal for God" (22:3). Moreover, the Risen Lord employs the language of popular philosophy in order to interpret Paul's persecution (26:14).

Consistent with the change of audience is the way in which Paul portrays himself in relationship to Judaism. While both Acts 22 and 26 argue for Paul's innocence with respect to the Jewish people, the arguments differ. As we have already seen, in chapter 22 Paul describes himself as a man who is firmly placed within the best tradition of his people by virtue of his birth, education, and zeal (v. 3). Even his call as a witness comes via a "devout" Jew, Ananias. The speech in chapter 26, by contrast, presents Paul as the victim of factionalism (v. 3), who is rejected because he affirms the resurrection. Both the beginning and the end of Paul's speech assert that it is Paul's belief in the resurrection of Jesus that has led to his arrest and trial.

Central to the structure of the speech in Acts 26 is Paul's encounter with Jesus and his response to that encounter (vv. 12–20). Although some students of Acts argue that the encounter serves the purpose of convincing Paul of the resurrection of Jesus, there is little in the encounter scene to support that conclusion. Indeed, here the encounter with Jesus is subsumed under Paul's call as "servant and witness." From the mouth of the Risen Lord comes the fullest description in Acts of Paul's task. Even the reference to what Paul has seen and will see is part of Paul's commission. It would be accurate to conclude that Acts 26 is not a conversion story, but a call story.

CONCLUSION

In Acts 9, 22, and 26 Luke describes the encounter between Paul and the Risen Lord that changed Paul from a persecutor of "the Way" into one of its most ardent proclaimers. Luke tells the story in a different manner each time, depending on the demands of the context. The first account, situated in a narrative about the movement of the church from Jerusalem to the gentile world and about the overcoming of the church's adversity, presents Paul as the enemy who is overthrown as he seeks to take persecution outside Jerusalem. The second account introduces Paul's defense speeches. Having been seized by his fellow Jews and charged with teaching against the people and the law and the temple (21:21, 28), Paul describes himself as a loyal Jew who was summoned by the "God of the Fathers" to witness to all people. The final account, which is also Paul's final defense speech, argues before Agrippa and Festus that Paul is persecuted simply because of a Jewish debate. Furthermore, the final account underscores Paul's call as witness and his faithful obedience to that call. In short, Luke tells the story of Paul's conversion in three different ways, each of which he has adapted very carefully to its narrative context. What Luke has is *one story,* or one tradition, which he has employed in different ways.

Because this is the case, it is not possible to isolate the earliest version of the story and it is certainly not possible to isolate the source of a particular version. At the outset of this chapter I mentioned earlier attempts to argue that Acts 9 derives from a Damascus source, Acts 26 from Paul, and that Acts 22 contains Luke's synthesis of the two. But this sort of analysis overlooks the Lukan vocabulary of all three accounts and the extent to which the demands of context have shaped the three versions. More recent attempts, such as those of Burchard, Löning, and Charles Hedrick, agree in isolating chapter 9 as the earliest version. It is true that the version of Acts 9, with its emphasis on the reversal of Paul the enemy rather than on his call, stands somewhat apart from 22 and 26. Once again, however, these differences derive from the place of the story within the narrative rather than from the proximity of chapter 9 to tradition.

Comparison of any one of these versions with the scanty comments made by Paul himself is problematic. To begin with, we must keep in mind the great differences between the two items being compared. While they are our only primary source, the comments in Paul's letters are just that—comments. Moreover, what Paul says reflects his own appropriation of events and an appropriation that is being used to make specific points with his correspondents. Luke, on the other hand, writes highly dramatic and engaging narratives; yet he is several decades removed from events and certainly uses the narratives to stress particular issues.

Perhaps it is not necessary to explore in detail all the ways in which Luke and Paul differ concerning Paul's conversion or transformation. The differences are so extensive that the similarities become impressive. Both describe Paul as having persecuted believers, although it is by no means clear that Paul refers to a legal and physical persecution. Both connect that revelation to a prophetic-like call to proclaim this gospel. (This is less prominent in Acts 9, but still present.) Both describe the amazement of believers that the persecutor now proclaims Jesus as Messiah (Gal. 1:23). These similarities are impressive. The two portraits have a similar shape, which suggests that Luke may have had access to a tradition about Paul's conversion.

There is, on the other hand, one major difference between these two that is not often articulated. Because Luke does tell of Paul's conversion three times, and at three significant points in the narrative, it appears that Luke understands the conversion to be definitive or constitutive of Paul. After all, Luke could have introduced Paul more briefly; he certainly could have defended Paul against the charges of false teaching without recourse to the conversion. The fact that this story appears three times, and fully told each time, suggests that, for Luke, the conversion itself is the determinative genesis of Paul's story. Henceforth, Paul remains the converted persecutor, and it is that reversal that should persuade people, Jews in particular, to hear him.

It is precisely at this point that Luke and Paul part company. Paul understands his experience to be an example of the reversal of values and expectations that is intrinsic to the New Age. He never dwells on the conversion in a way that would suggest that it is somehow definitive of himself.

To say that Luke understands the conversion to be definitive of Paul is not to say that Luke understands Paul to be the prototypical or paradigmatic convert. That is, the conversion of Paul may be definitive of Luke's view of Paul but not of Luke's view of conversion. Nothing in Luke's narrative suggests that other converts are to follow Paul's pattern or that Paul follows some Lukan pattern of conversion.

Although Paul is not a paradigmatic convert, there are certain assumptions operative in Luke's narrative that are important to note: (1) Paul's conversion results from divine initiative; (2) conversion is not an end in itself but a means to the growth of the gospel; (3) the narratives we have examined treat an individual conversion, but not an individualistic conversion, since Paul is not converted in order to savor the experience but always in order to witness. One question in chapter 3 will be whether these conclusions hold true throughout Luke's two-volume work.

NOTES

1. The name "Luke" is used here simply because it is the traditional designation of the author of the third Gospel and the Acts of the Apostles.

2. See, for example, F. C. Baur, *Paul*, 2d ed., 2 vols., ed. Eduard Zeller, trans. A. Menzies (London: Williams & Norgate, 1875–76), 1: 68, 71–72; Johannes Weiss, *History of Primitive Christianity,* 2 vols., completed by

Rudolf Knopf, ed. F. C. Grant, trans. F. C. Grant, et al. (New York: Wilson-Erickson, 1937), 186–94.

3. An excellent example is A. C. McGiffert, *A History of Christianity in the Apostolic Age,* rev. ed. (New York: Charles Scribner's Sons, 1906), 119–209.

4. Emanuel Hirsch, "Die drei Berichte der Apostelgeschichte über die Bekehrung des Paulus," *ZNW* 29 (1929): 305–12.

5. Hans Conzelmann, *The Theology of St. Luke,* trans. G. Buswell (Philadelphia: Fortress Press, 1982 [1953]). Christoph Burchard, *Der dreizehnte Zeuge: Traditions—und kompositions-geschichtliche Untersuchungen zu Lukas' Darstellung der Frühzeit des Paulus,* FRLANT 103 (Göttingen: Vandenhoeck & Ruprecht, 1970), 119–22. Similar conclusions are drawn by Charles W. Hedrick in "Paul's Conversion/Call," *JBL* 100 (1981): 415–32.

6. Karl Löning, *Der Saulustradition in der Apostelgeschichte,* NTAbh 9 (Münster: Verlag Aschendorff, 1973), 18–19.

7. On the contrast here see Burchard, *Der dreizehnte Zeuge,* 40. It should be noted that the RSV may exaggerate the contrast between 8:2 and 8:3 by translating the *de* at the beginning of v. 3 with "but." However, *de* may be either conjunctive or disjunctive; moreover, *de* also appears at the beginning of 8:1a, 1b, and 2. 8:2 and 8:3 are contrasting notices, but that is because of the content of the verses, not because of the *de.*

8. Abraham Malherbe has pointed out to me that Luke treats the figure of Barnabas in a comparable fashion. Luke introduces Barnabas in Acts 4:36 as "son of consolation," but says little else about him. When Barnabas reappears in 9:27, however, he acts in accordance with the earlier description by easing Paul's way with the Jerusalem Christians.

9. For other connections between these two conversion narratives, see below, pp. 123–24.

10. 9:31 is one of the summary statements that Luke uses in order to mark transitions in the narrative.

11. Although *apeilē* ("threat") occurs only two other times in the New Testament (Acts 4:29 and Eph. 6:9), and in the LXX normally refers to the power of God (cf. Hab. 3:12; Isa. 50:2), it does appear frequently in 3 and 4 Maccabees, where it refers to the threat from the king or the king's agent against those Jews who are faithful to God (cf. 3 Macc. 2:24; 5:18; 5:37; 4 Macc. 4:8; 7:2; 8:19).

12. Commentators have frequently offered elaborate explanations of how Christians came to be in Damascus at this time, since Luke has not previously mentioned Damascus. Such explanations miss the point Luke is making, which is that Paul's persecution has reached its zenith; it now extends even into the Diaspora.

13. *En* plus the articular infinitive and *egeneto* plus the infinitive are both

frequent constructions in Luke-Acts, as in the LXX. What is unusual here is that the two constructions appear together.

14. For a more thorough discussion of *diōkein*, see above, pp. 25–26.

15. Ernst Haenchen, *The Acts of the Apostles* (Philadelphia: Westminster Press, 1971), 322.

16. Unlike *de*, which may be either conjunctive or disjunctive, *alla* is normally disjunctive.

17. Paul Schubert, "The Structure and Significance of Luke 24," *Neutestamentlichen Studien für Rudolf Bultmann*, ed. W. Eltester (Berlin: Alfred Töpelmann, 1954), 181; Luke T. Johnson, *The Literary Function of Possessions in Luke-Acts*, SBLDS (Missoula, Mont.: Scholars Press, 1977), 15–16; J. A. Fitzmyer, *The Gospel According to Luke I–IX* (Garden City, N.Y.: Doubleday & Co., 1981), 179–80.

18. Haenchen, *Acts*, 323.

19. W. C. van Unnik reminds us that *idou* is used to call attention to what follows, to introduce something new or unexpected ("Der Befehl an Philippus," *Sparsa Collecta*, 3 vols. (Leiden: E. J. Brill, 1973), 1: 335–37.

20. Löning, *Die Saulustradition*, 30–31.

21. Paul Schubert, "The Final Cycle of Speeches in the Book of Acts," *JBL* 87 (1968): 7.

22. Haenchen, *Acts*, 325.

23. It is true that Luke elsewhere distinguishes baptism and the reception of the Spirit as two stages. For example, the Samaritans are baptized by Philip, but must receive the Holy Spirit from the apostles (8:12–17). However, Luke does not have a rigid system which applies in every instance. In Acts 9, Saul's actions in vv. 19–22 indicate that he has received all that is needed.

24. Certainly scene 5 is complex, but from the standpoint of the story of Paul's encounter with Jesus, vv. 19b–30 make one major point and cannot be divided into several parts.

25. See above, n. 8.

26. Frederick Veltmann, "The Defense Speeches of Paul in Acts" (Ph.D. diss., Graduate Theological Union, 1975), 209.

27. Van Unnik has demonstrated that this statement conforms to a standard formula ("Tarsus or Jerusalem," *Sparsa Collecta*, 1: 321–27).

28. Haenchen, *Acts*, 625.

29. Luke 18:37; Acts 2:22; 3:6; 4:10; 6:14; 22:8; 24:5; 26:9.

30. Haenchen, *Acts*, 626.

31. This is not to imply that Luke regarded Paul as an apostle, since the qualifications of Acts 1:21–22 exclude him from that category.

32. Martin Dibelius, *Studies in the Acts of the Apostles*, trans. Mary Ling (London: SCM Press; New York: Charles Scribner's Sons, 1956), 160–61, comments that the interruption is a "literary device" used in order to draw attention to the main point of the speech.

33. Schubert ("Final Cycle of Speeches," 8) writes that Paul's speech in Acts 26 "rounds out and unifies the double aim of the Book of Acts—Luke's intention to set forth his theology in the speeches and to clinch the significance of Paul." See also Robert F. O'Toole, *Acts 26: The Christological Climax of Paul's Defense (Acts 22:1—26:32),* AnBib 78 (Rome: Biblical Institute Press, 1978), 156.

34. Presumably the RSV reads as it does because verbs of speaking often occur in the imperfect, but in Acts there are many instances in which verbs of speaking appear in the aorist tense, especially at the beginning of speeches (e.g., 1:15; 2:14; 13:16; 15:7; 21:40; 23:1; 24:10). Hence, it is possible that 26:2–23 continues a defense that actually began in Acts 22. The continuity of 22 and 26 was suggested to me on other grounds by Vernon Robbins, letter dated 3 May 1983.

35. Veltmann, "The Defense Speeches of Paul in Acts," 218–21.

36. Haenchen, *Acts,* 691.

37. See Pindar, *Pythian Odes,* 2.94–95; Aeschylus, *Agamemnon,* 1624, *Prometheus,* 324–25; Euripides, *Bacchae,* 794–95.

38. K. H. Rengstorf, *"hypēretēs," TDNT* 8: 542–43.

39. B and C* are among the major witnesses for the inclusion of *me. me* is omitted by p[74], ℵ, A, and C[2]. The 26th edition of the Nestle text retains *me* in the text, but in brackets. The third edition of the UBS Greek NT likewise indicates considerable doubt about the reading. It seems probable that a scribe was perplexed by the meaning of "the things which you saw," and wrote *me* in the margin in order to explain what it was that Paul saw. Later scribes moved *me* into the text itself.

40. Cf. Philo, *On the Virtues,* 179.

41. The one place in Luke's gospel where *epistrephein* occurs poses an interesting exception to this usage. In Luke 1:16 Zechariah is told that John will turn the people of Israel to God. For this reason, and based on the grammatical ambiguity, we cannot rule out the possibility that it is Paul who is to turn people "from darkness to light." That translation would only heighten the stress that Acts 26 places on the servanthood of Paul.

CHAPTER 3

"What God Has Cleansed"

*Conversion in
Luke-Acts (Part 2)*

Luke's interest in conversion is by no means limited to the narratives about Paul. Indeed, in the opening of Luke's Gospel he characterizes John the Baptist as one who "will turn (*epistrephein*) many of the sons of Israel to the Lord their God" (Luke 1:16). When Jesus is presented in the temple, Simeon speaks of Jesus as God's salvation, "a light for revelation to the Gentiles" (Luke 2:32; cf. Isa. 42:6; 49:6).[1] At the conclusion of the Gospel and again at the beginning of Acts, Jesus announces that the gospel will be preached to all people (Luke 24:46–48; Acts 1:8). Acts itself contains both notices about the conversions of large groups of people and stories about conversions of individuals.

Because of the rich texture of Luke's narrative garment, students of Luke have found it difficult to arrive at an adequate assessment of Luke's treatment of conversion. Often Luke's view of conversion is reduced to his use of particular words such as *metanoun* and *epistrephein*.[2] This approach describes the texture of Luke's garment by means of a few threads. However prominent those threads are, they do not of themselves constitute the garment. That observation is particularly important in this instance, since *epistrephein* and *metanoun* appear in Luke-Acts in ways that conform to their conventional usage.[3]

Others arrive at Luke's view of conversion by examining the patterns followed by various persons or groups who become part of the community of believers.[4] Often Peter's statement in Acts 2:38 is taken to reflect Luke's scheme of conversion ("Repent, and be baptized every one of you in the name of the Lord Jesus for the forgiveness of your sins; and you shall receive the gift of the Holy Spirit"), and that scheme becomes the basis for analyzing conversions that occur elsewhere in Acts. The problem with this approach is that it selects one small pattern in the garment and seeks to make the rest of the garment conform to that pattern.

Luke's rich garment can never be described by reference to a few of its threads or one of its striking patterns. To get at Luke's understanding of conversion, or his *understandings*, we need to attend to the early stories of mass conversions, and we need to give special attention to his developed stories about individual converts, because Luke himself has seen fit to tell those stories at considerable length.[5] Since we have already examined the conversion of Paul, we will focus here especially on the stories of the Ethiopian eunuch and Cornelius. Important for this inquiry is what Luke says about the individual's conversion, but also how that conversion relates to other conversions in Acts and how individual stories function within the larger narrative.

CONVERSION OF THE MASSES

Discussion of conversion in Acts rightly begins with the conclusion of Peter's speech at Pentecost. The crowd is moved to ask Peter and his colleagues what they should do to respond to Peter's words. Peter answers,

> Repent, and be baptized every one of you in the name of Jesus Christ for the forgiveness of your sins; and you shall receive the gift of the Holy Spirit. For the promise is to you and to your children and to all that are far off, everyone whom the Lord our God calls to him. (Acts 2:38–39)

At first glance, it seems reasonable to regard v. 38 as Luke's statement of the pattern of conversion. One who is "cut to the heart" (v. 37) repents, is baptized, receives forgiveness of sins, and then receives the Holy Spirit. The difficulty with this assessment of 2:38, as noted earlier, is that it forces one pattern on all the texts. Nowhere else in Acts does this pattern of conversion appear. When Luke refers to groups of converts, he says simply that many believed (4:4; 5:14; 9:42) or many turned to the Lord (9:35). None of the three lengthy stories about individual converts conforms to this pattern, as we shall see.

What we find in 2:38 is not an order of salvation (*ordo salutis*), but an effective conclusion to Peter's speech. Addressing Jerusalemites, Peter has emphasized their culpability in the crucifixion of Jesus: "Jesus of Nazareth, a man attested to you by God . . . this Jesus . . . you crucified and killed by the hands of lawless men" (2:22–23). The last line of the speech reiterates this point: "Let all the house of Israel therefore know assuredly that God has made him both Lord and Christ, this Jesus whom you crucified" (2:36). Peter insists that those who hear him are guilty. When they ask what they must do, therefore, the context itself dictates that Peter call for repentance and promise forgiveness of sins. Certainly repentance and forgiveness appear in other speeches in Acts (3:19; 13:38; 17:30), but they have a special appropriateness here.

In addition to being an effective conclusion to Peter's speech, 2:38 provides a transition to the ensuing narrative of the expansion of the Jerusalem community. Peter's audience responds overwhelmingly to his call for repentance and baptism (2:41–42). Although Peter and the other apostles quickly encounter opposition from the authorities, these early chapters are dominated by the growth of the community, its unity, and its divine protection and power.

Within these early chapters of Acts, then, references to conversion appear in Luke's portrait of the community's growth and its favor with God. The number of those added indicates to the reader that Gamaliel's words are being fulfilled. The community is from God and cannot be overthrown (5:39).

Stephen's martyrdom constitutes a break in the narrative (6:8—8:1a). Persecution against the Jerusalem community follows Stephen's death and forces most believers out into Judea and Samaria where they proclaim the gospel (8:1b–4).[6] This movement into Judea and Samaria marks fulfillment of the second part of Jesus' pronouncement in 1:8. The church has begun its movement to "the end of the earth." It is at this crucial point that Luke introduces the first story of the conversion of an individual.[7]

THE ETHIOPIAN EUNUCH

Very early in the history of the church, a tradition arose that the Ethiopian eunuch whom Philip baptized returned to his home country and there proclaimed the gospel.[8] While the text itself says nothing about the eunuch becoming an evangelist, it is easy to understand why readers would draw such a conclusion. The story of the highly placed Ethiopian official who suddenly appears, responds, and goes on his way, elicits the enthusiastic—perhaps even imaginative—response of an audience.

In addition to eliciting enthusiasm, the conversion of the Ethiopian eunuch has elicited considerable confusion, particularly regarding the origin of the story and its relationship to the Cornelius narrative in Acts 10. How did Luke obtain this story? More important, since the eunuch is surely to be regarded as a Gentile, why does Luke present Cornelius as the first Gentile convert?

Adolf von Harnack argued that the story itself came from Philip. Because we read later on that Philip's daughters had prophetic gifts (Acts 21:8–9), Harnack concluded that Philip also had a "pneumato-scientific" disposition, which explained the miraculous elements in the story. Luke is thus simply passing on the story he has received from Philip.[9]

At the other extreme, Martin Dibelius characterized the narrative as a legend. He observed that it combines miraculous elements, devotional elements (readings from the Scripture), and personal elements (information concerning the eunuch), all of which commonly occur in legends. Further, Dibelius suggested that short stories of actual conversions, told without reference to principle, circulated within the early church.[10] This means that the origin of the story is completely lost.

More recently Ernst Haenchen has argued that the history of the story is complex. He concurs with Dibelius that it comes from church tradition but, because it features Philip as protagonist, Haenchen regards the story as a product of Hellenistic Christians, specifically of "communities founded by the Seven." Haenchen also argues that this was the Hellenistic Christian account of the first conversion of a Gentile. Luke was unwilling to present it as such, because Luke was underscoring the role of the apostles, and Philip rather than Peter had baptized the eunuch. The story was widely known, however, and Luke could not simply omit it. Thus, he includes it as "an edifying story . . . illustrating the progress of the mission."[11]

As different as these three treatments of Acts 8:26–40 are, they all are concerned primarily with the history of the narrative. While that is a legitimate task, our study of the narratives of Paul's conversion has already demonstrated that preoccupation with the history of the text may prevent us from seeing the dynamics within the text and the relationship between this text and the larger narrative. Only after we have given attention to the narrative itself can we ask about its origin and history.

There is much within this particular narrative that calls for our attention. We will look first at Philip's commission and his response, then at the identity of the eunuch and his actions, and finally at the encounter of the two and the aftermath of that encounter.

> But an angel of the Lord said to Philip, "Rise and go toward the south to the road that goes down from Jerusalem to Gaza." This is a desert road. And he rose and went. And behold, an Ethiopian, a eunuch, a minister of Candace, the queen of the Ethiopians, in charge of all her treasure, had come to Jerusalem to worship and was returning; seated in his chariot, he was reading the prophet Isaiah. And the spirit said to Philip, "Go up and join this chariot." So Philip ran to him, and heard him reading Isaiah the prophet, and asked, "Do you understand what you are reading?" And he said, "How can I, unless some one guides me?" And he invited Philip to come up and sit with him. Now the passage of the scripture which he was reading was this:
> "As a sheep led to the slaughter
> or a lamb before its shearer is dumb,
> so he opens not his mouth.
> In his humiliation justice was
>   denied him.
> Who can describe his generation?
> For his life is taken up from the
>   earth."
> And the eunuch said to Philip, "About whom, pray, does the prophet say this, about himself or about some one else?" Then Philip opened his mouth, and beginning with this scripture he told him the good news of Jesus. And as they went along the eunuch said, "See, here is water! What is to prevent my being baptized?" And he commanded the chariot to stop, and they both went down into the water, Philip and the eunuch, and he baptized him. And when they came up out of the water, the Spirit of the Lord caught up Philip; and the eunuch saw him no more, and went on his way rejoicing. But Philip was found at Azotus, and passing on he preached the gospel to all the towns till he came to Caesarea. (Acts 8:26–40)

The story begins as the logical continuation of Philip's work in Samaria. When believers in Jerusalem fled the city, Philip went to Samaria, where many responded to his preaching (8:5–13). News of this response reached Jerusalem, and Peter and John went down so that those who believed might receive the Holy Spirit (8:14–17). After their encounter with Simon Magus (8:18–24), we read this: "Now when they had testified and spoken the word of the Lord, they returned to Jerusalem, preaching the gospel to many villages of the Samaritans" (8:25).

What do we expect to find next in the narrative? Because the "they" of v. 25 is left unspecified, we might suppose that Philip returned to Jerusalem along with Peter and John. However, we will soon learn that that is not the case. The activity of Peter and John is distinct from that of Philip. We might also notice that v. 25 begins with the word *men*, and that *de* stands at the beginning of v. 26. When used successively in this way, *men* and *de* can be translated "on the one hand" and "on the other hand." If we read v. 25 carefully, then ("On the one hand, they") we might expect to find that v. 26 begins with some reference to Philip: "On the other hand, Philip stayed behind," or "on the other hand, Philip went first to Jerusalem." Instead, we read this: "On the other hand, an angel of the Lord. . . ." Our expectation has been soundly thwarted.[12]

Not only does an angel appear when the narrative has prepared us to expect some action by Philip, but the angel's order is itself unexpected, even absurd. The angel tells Philip to arise and go down a deserted road in the middle of the day!

Because the RSV translates part of v. 26 differently, some explanation is required here. The Greek phrase, which is translated "toward the south" in the RSV, is *kata mesēmbrian*, and it can mean either "about midday" or "toward the south." Despite the fact that the phrase regularly appears in the Septuagint as a reference to time (e.g., Gen. 18:1; 43:16; Deut. 28:29; 1 Kings 18:26–27; Jer. 6:4), most commentators insist that here direction ("toward the south") is intended. Their reason is that the noonday sun makes traveling extremely difficult in the Middle East, something to be avoided if at all possible.[13]

It appears, however, that Luke did not know that no one travels at noon, for in Acts 22:6 and 26:13 Paul explicitly says that his encounter with Jesus occurred as he and his companions were traveling during the middle of the day! Although the wording does not exactly duplicate 8:26, the meaning is clearly that Paul was on the road around noontime. Although such travel is generally to be avoided, Luke does include it, and in both cases a startling event follows.[14]

The angel not only directs Philip to set out at the worst time of day, but toward an unlikely spot. Philip is to go on "the road that goes down from Jerusalem to Gaza. This is a desert road."[15] "Desert" translates the Greek word *erēmos*, which also means desolate or empty. The command of the angel ends here. Philip, who has just finished a great work of proclaiming the word in Samaria to "the multitudes" (8:6), now finds himself directed to a deserted place at a time when no one would be present! Luke's point lies in the very absurdity of the order.[16] As is the case elsewhere in Acts, God commands the unexpected, even the ridiculous (e.g., 5:20; 9:12; 10:9–16).

Throughout v. 26, we read only of the angel's directions. Philip says nothing. One brief sentence at the beginning of v. 27 describes his response: "And he rose and went."[17] Despite the absurdity of the angel's demand, Philip complies. This obedience characterizes Philip's actions throughout the story. He responds to directions and inquiries, but takes no action without being prompted. Philip sets out as he has been told (v. 27). In v. 29 the Spirit tells him to go and join the chariot of the eunuch, and he does so. In v. 30 he ventures to ask the eunuch, who is already reading, whether he understands what he reads. In v. 35 he responds to the eunuch's question about Scripture and preaches Jesus to him. Even this action became muted, however, by the action of the eunuch. Verse 38 explains that Philip baptized the eunuch, but immediately thereafter Philip is seized by the Spirit and finds himself at Azotus.

Although commentators describe Philip as the protagonist of this narrative, his action is largely that of acquiescence. Haenchen contrasts the story of Philip's great deeds in Samaria with this story in which Philip "scarcely acts at all, and is rather represented as the guided instrument of God."[18] Haenchen's conclusion, as noted earlier, is that Luke deliberately suppresses the story, but that conclusion falters when we look more closely at the real protagonist of the story.

Just after Philip's compliance with the angel's command, we encounter the Ethiopian, who is introduced in considerable detail in Acts 8:27b–28:

> ... and behold, an Ethiopian, a eunuch, a minister of Candace, the queen of the Ethiopians, in charge of all her treasure, had come to Jerusalem to worship and was returning; seated in his chariot, he was reading the prophet Isaiah.

We should not overlook the way in which Luke announces the Ethiopian. "And behold!" (*kai idou*) appears in the Bible so frequently that we may overlook it. Often the expression is used to call for particular attention or to denote that something new and unexpected follows.[19] In this context "and behold!" seems particularly apt. Philip has embarked at an unpromising hour to an uninhabited place and finds someone who is quite extraordinary. The description of this person warrants our attention.

Luke first describes the person whom Philip sees as a male Ethiopian. That he is an Ethiopian would in itself arouse considerable interest on the part of Luke's audience. In the Greco-Roman world the term "Ethiopian" was applied to anyone who was dark-skinned, but especially to those who came from lands south of Egypt.[20] Moreover, Greek writers showed considerable interest in Ethiopians.[21] The Odyssey speaks of the "far-off Ethiopians . . . , the farthermost of men" (1.22–23). Herodotus describes them as the tallest and most handsome of all the peoples (3.17–20). Strabo's description of the Ethiopians, written not many decades prior to Luke-Acts, remarks that they came from the "extremities of the inhabited world" (*ta akra tēs oikoumenēs*, 17.2,1–3). Similarly, in the Old Testament and in the writings of the church fathers, the Ethiopian is one who comes from the borders of the known world.[22]

Luke's character is not only an Ethiopian, but an official of "Candace, the queen of the Ethiopians." That is, he comes from Meroe, a kingdom that had been established and powerful since before the time of Alexander the Great, and one whose queens traditionally bore the title "Candace."[23] Luke's contemporaries would have been particularly interested in an agent of the ruler of Meroe. Late in the first century B.C., Augustus's General Gaius Petronius had led a military campaign against the Candace's army when Ethiopians pushed into Elephantine.[24] In addition, there had been scientific expeditions into Meroe under Nero around A.D. 62, and Nero had planned though never executed a military campaign against Meroe.[25]

This particular Ethiopian, we are told, happens to be a eunuch. Interpreters have customarily given considerable attention to this fact, because it implies that the Ethiopian is to be regarded as a Gentile and not as a Jew or a proselyte. Certainly that position appears in Deut. 23:1 and it is maintained in Josephus (*Antiquities* 4.290–91). After we have looked at the total description of this individual, we can better assess Luke's view of him. It is sufficient for now to note that Luke does not emphasize the fact that this is a eunuch. Philip makes no pronouncement about his status and raises no objection to him. After this long introduction, however, Luke's way of referring to him is consistently to speak of "the eunuch" (vv. 34, 36, 38, 39).

As was frequently the case, the eunuch occupied a position of power and authority. Indeed, if Luke did not describe the man as a eunuch *and* as a minister of Candace, we might conclude that he was simply a court official and not physically a eunuch at all.[26] That he controls all the treasury of Meroe means that this is indeed a well-placed and significant person.

Because the eunuch is almost certainly to be regarded as a Gentile, Luke's comment at the end of v. 27 is puzzling: the eunuch had come to Jerusalem in order to worship. Some have concluded from this that he is a proselyte or a God-fearer. There are, however, indications that Gentiles worshiped in the Jerusalem temple.[27] Moreover, the popular mind seems to have viewed both Ethiopians and eunuchs as especially sensitive to religious matters. Thus, worshiping in Jerusalem merely indicates the receptivity of this particular individual.

Having been to Jerusalem, the eunuch now returns and is reading along the way.[28] What is at first perplexing here is that the eunuch has in his possession and is reading a scroll that contains at least a passage from Isaiah. Again, some have concluded from this detail that the eunuch must have been a proselyte, because a mere God-fearer could not have acquired such a scroll, but such a conclusion fails to see the function of the scroll in the text. The eunuch reads from the scroll and thus provides Philip (or the Holy Spirit) with an opportunity for approaching the eunuch.

With the Spirit's prompting of Philip at the beginning of v. 29, the introduction of the eunuch comes to a close. He by no means recedes into the background, however. Quite in contrast to Philip, who quietly acquiesces to the directions given him, the eunuch emerges as a main actor. In v. 31 he seeks help from Philip by confessing that he needs an interpreter and by inviting Philip to join him. He then asks Philip to interpret the text that he has been reading (v. 34). Most important, it is the eunuch who asks for baptism and who, without waiting for Philip's answer,[29] orders the chariot to stop so that he may be baptized.

The person who emerges from Luke's narrative is not someone whom Luke has included only grudgingly. He is, instead, a powerful representative of those who exist at the geographical limits of Luke's world. He is also one who, as a eunuch, exists beyond the boundaries of the Jewish religious communities. Nevertheless, he reaches out to be included even as God directs that same inclusion.

The meeting between Philip and the Ethiopian eunuch moves quickly to that inclusion. As noted above, the meeting begins when Philip asks whether the eunuch understands what he is reading.[30] The eunuch's response, which confesses neither his dullness nor his ignorance, indicates his eagerness and provides the setting for the citation from Isaiah 53 that follows.[31] Many questions might be raised regarding the Scripture, but the eunuch seizes on one that is central: To whom does this text refer? Philip's response to the question is to proclaim Jesus.

Without specifying the content of Philip's remarks or their impact on the eunuch, Luke moves immediately to the eunuch's request for baptism: "What is to prevent my being baptized?" (*kōlyein*, v. 36). This question recurs later on in the Cornelius narrative, when Peter concludes finally that he cannot prevent baptism for the Gentiles (*kōlyein*, 10:47; 11:17). Here in Acts 8, some later scribes felt it necessary that Philip provide an answer to the eunuch's question, in the form of a faith requirement. But that requirement belongs to later tradition and not to Luke, who follows the eunuch's question with his baptism.

Immediately following the eunuch's baptism, the Spirit seizes Philip, who lands in Azotus and there begins to proclaim the gospel. Of the eunuch we read only that he "went on his way rejoicing" (v. 39b). His response, then, is comparable to that which Luke ascribes to Gentiles elsewhere in Acts when they learn of their own reception by the community (13:48; 15:31; cf. also 5:41; 11:23).

What are we to make of this unique story? Surely we cannot be content with discussing its possible origins. Wherever Luke obtained the story, and that question may be unanswerable, he has crafted it into a powerful narrative. Haenchen's suggestion that Luke is *suppressing* a tradition in which Philip converts the first Gentile seems odd when we see how Luke has underscored and emphasized the story—not suppressed it!

We might suppose that this is a story regarding an ideal or a typical conversion. F. F. Bruce seems to regard it in that way. Bruce argues that the eunuch must have learned something about the Christian faith elsewhere, or that Philip ended his proclamation in the same way Peter concluded his Pentecost discourse (2:38).[32] That is, Bruce assumes that the conversion of the Ethiopian must have followed the conversion pattern established at Pentecost. But nothing in the story allows for that conclusion! According to Luke, the pivot of the conversation between Philip and the eunuch was the identity of the figure referred to in the Isaiah text. Philip preached Jesus (v. 35). We hear nothing of a call to repentance or a promise of the forgiveness of sins as in Acts 2:38.

That is because the Ethiopian eunuch is not a typical convert but a *symbolic* convert. He does not establish a pattern that later conversions must follow. Instead, as one who comes from the limits of Luke's geographical world (an Ethiopian) and beyond Luke's religious community (a eunuch), he symbolizes all those whose inclusion has been announced in Acts 1:8. It may be that Luke has in mind here the fulfillment of and hence the overturning of the legal exclusion of the eunuch, but the story is not limited to those laws and their reversal.

When we ponder the story of the Ethiopian eunuch in light of the typology of conversion outlined in chapter 1, we encounter significant difficulties. Since Luke enhances the mysterious nature of the eunuch's identity, we learn little that falls appropriately into a conversion type. We do not know how the eunuch subsequently assessed his own past, and, thus, we cannot classify this either as a pendulum-like conversion or as a transformation. Given the fact that the eunuch is described as one who has worshiped in Jerusalem and who reads

Scripture, it is possible that what the eunuch experiences is an alternation. His request for baptism continues a quest on which he has been embarked for some time.

In conventional interpretations, the story of the Ethiopian eunuch is seen as a kind of addendum to Philip's ministry among the Samaritans. After entering Samaria, Philip happens to encounter an Ethiopian and baptizes him. But that reading of the story overlooks the unique beginning of the story and the astonishing character of the Ethiopian. It also ignores the relationship between this conversion and the conversions that follow in Acts 9 and 10. We can best assess that relationship following our discussion of the Cornelius account in Acts 10.

CORNELIUS—OR PETER?

The conversions of Samaritans, the Ethiopian eunuch, and the persecutor Saul provide the reader of Acts with a clear signal that the mission inaugurated at Pentecost does not belong to the Jews of Jerusalem or Judea. On the contrary, God has reached out to one from "the ends of the earth" and to one who had been "the enemy." In this way Luke sets the stage for the narrative of Peter and Cornelius.

Between the conversion of Saul and the Cornelius account Luke includes two other episodes, in each of which Peter is central. Because both episodes describe miracles (the healing of Aeneas in Acts 9:32–35 and the resurrection of Dorcas in 9:36–43), we might suppose that they are unrelated to the conversion narrative that follows. These brief stories are also narratives of conversion, however. The healing of Aeneas concludes with a notice that all those living in Lydda and Sharon "turned to the Lord" (9:35). In the same way, Tabitha's resurrection "became known throughout all Joppa, and many believed in the Lord" (9:42). The last section of Acts 9 thus reintroduces Peter and further prepares for the events of Acts 10.

As is the case with many important issues in Acts, the work of Dibelius has dominated interpretation of the Cornelius account. Dibelius argued that the Cornelius narrative was based on an earlier "simple" legend, similar to the legend of the Ethiopian eunuch. Beginning with this assumption, Dibelius isolated those elements in the story that conflict with the original, particularly those in which there is some reference to questions of principle. The result is that Dibelius regarded the following as Lukan additions: Peter's vision in 10:9–16, which may be an actual experience of Peter, although not originally connected with this episode; the awkward description of Peter's arrival at Caesarea in 10:27–29; Peter's sermon (10:34–43), which would not have been included in a simple conversion legend and which conforms to the pattern of Peter's other speeches; and the recapitulation in Jerusalem (11:1–18), because it centers on Peter's association with Gentiles, an element that is insignificant in the story itself.[33]

Most studies of the Cornelius narrative since Dibelius have offered relatively minor adjustments to his thesis. Haenchen questioned Dibelius's assumption that the early church collected conversion stories, but his own thesis was that Luke received the Cornelius narrative (largely as Dibelius had described it) from a Caesarea tradition. Haenchen also argued that Luke himself had created the story of Peter's vision in order to explain 10:28.[34] Ulrich Wilckens criticized Dibelius's claim that Peter's speech in 10:34–43 is like other speeches in Luke-Acts, noting that this speech is catechetical rather than kerygmatic.[35] Francois Bovon insisted that the vision of Peter and the discussion in Jerusalem (11:1–18) together formed a second tradition that had to do with the demise of the food laws. According to Bovon, Luke interpreted this tradition figuratively, as 10:28 and 10:34–35 indicate.[36] Karl Löning contended that the vision of Peter was an indispensable part of the early Cornelius tradition.[37]

None of these studies examines carefully the assumptions behind Dibelius's work. More radical analysis has recently been undertaken by Klaus Haacker, who underscores Dibelius's assumption that the Cornelius story was originally a short and simple conversion narrative. The only parallel to which Dibelius can point, however, is the narrative of the Ethiopian eunuch. And Haacker notes, as we have already seen, that the narrative of the eunuch is by no means a simple story told without reference to principle![38] Haacker thus dismantles one major piece of Dibelius's work—his assumption that Luke's source is an earlier and "simpler" story.

The pivotal issue in Dibelius's thesis is whether the narrative of Cornelius existed without Peter's vision in 10:9–16. Are these two separate traditions that Luke has clumsily wed to one another? At first glance, there do appear to be reasons to think that Peter's vision is extrinsic, added either prior to Luke or by Luke himself. After all, the vision does not have any *explicit* connection with the surrounding story, since the vision pertains to food laws, not to the inclusion of a pious Gentile.

There are, on the other hand, factors that counterbalance and indeed outweigh these initial observations. An examination of certain narrative practices in Luke's world, combined with careful attention to the story itself, will show that the vision of Peter is integral to the narrative. While he may have known a tradition about Peter and a well-placed Gentile, the shape and extent of that tradition is no longer accessible to us. The narrative that stands in Acts 10:1—11:18 was written entirely by Luke and reflects his concerns at every point. These concerns are several, but one that is overlooked as a result of Dibelius's work is the connection between the conversion of Cornelius and the issue of *hospitality*, the sharing of food and shelter between Jews and Gentiles. By means of the issue of *hospitality*, Luke demonstrates that the conversion of the first Gentile required the conversion of the church as well. Indeed, in Luke's account, Peter and company undergo a change that is more wrenching by far than the change experienced by Cornelius.

We begin with Dibelius's literary argument, which overlooks the fact that there are numerous narratives in the Greco-Roman world in which, as in Acts 10, two characters experience separate dreams or visions as aspects of one episode. For example, when Josephus describes Alexander's sacrifice at the temple at Jerusalem, Alexander and the high priest each have a dream in which they are prepared for the events that follow (*Antiquities* 11.321–39). As in Acts 10, the dreams are not the same but they complement each other and enhance the narrative. Alfred Wikenhauser collected some fifteen texts in which there are "double visions," as in Acts 10.[39] That this phenomenon is not foreign to Luke is confirmed, of course, by the double vision of Ananias and Saul in Acts 9. The presence of these double visions elsewhere should make us cautious about assuming that Peter's vision has been inserted into an earlier and simpler narrative.

The central issue, however, involves the relationship between the content of Peter's vision and the context of the larger narrative. Peter's vision contains no explicit connection to the question of admitting Gentiles, nor does the vision contain a direct order about Gentiles (cf. Acts 16:9). One way of pursuing this issue is to ask whether there are other narratives in Luke-Acts, or in literature that would have been familiar to Luke or contemporary with Luke, in which there are visions or dreams the significance of which becomes clear only as the narrative unfolds. If there are such, then the possibility increases that the unclarity around Peter's vision is part of the narrative itself and not a byproduct of connecting two separate and unrelated traditions.

Luke-Acts contains a number of annunciations and visions. While these sometimes elicit surprise on the part of the person to whom the annunciation or vision comes (e.g., Luke 1:11–12, 26–29), the meaning of the vision is usually clear when it occurs. Nevertheless, these visions and revelations vary greatly from one another, and any generalization about them would be perilous (apart from the obvious comment that they mark some significant turn of events).

Narratives in the Hebrew Bible frequently involve dreams or visions, and here we find some potential parallels to Acts 10. Pharaoh's dream about the cows and the grain takes on meaning only after Joseph interprets it (Genesis 41). Similarly, only Daniel's interpretations bring out the importance of Nebuchadnezzar's dreams (Dan. 2:31–45; 4:1–27) and of the writing on Belshazzar's wall (Dan. 5:5–28). In these narratives, however, the quest to understand the dream dominates the story in a way unlike Acts 10 and thus the parallels to Acts 10 are not convincing.

We find closer parallels to Acts 10 in the writings of Plutarch and in the Hellenistic romances. In Plutarch's life of Brutus, Cinna dreams that Caesar has invited him to dinner. On the following day Cinna attends Caesar's funeral and is destroyed by those who take him to be Caesar's enemy (*Brutus* 20.8–11). Plutarch also describes a dream of Cicero's, in which Cicero sees Octavius, whom he had never met. The next day Cicero does in fact meet Octavius (*Cicero* 44). In these and other instances (*Cimon* 18; *Lucullus* 10; 23.3–4), dreams become meaningful only as the narrative progresses.

The Hellenistic romances also employ dreams in this way. Very early on in Achilles Tatius's story, *Leucippe and Clitophon*, Clitophon dreams of being attached to a wife and then severed by someone else (1.3). The dream is fulfilled in the sense that Clitophon's engagement to Calligone is broken, but the dream is further fulfilled when Clitophon and Leucippe are separated by a series of tragic circumstances. Similarly, *The Ephesian Tale* of Xenophon contains a dream of Habrocomes, in which a huge woman sets fire to the ship in which he and his bride, Anthia, are sailing. The dream concludes when Habrocomes and Anthia swim to safety, and the narrator comments that Habrocomes is disturbed by the dream. Habrocomes' dream is not fulfilled in the narrative. Nevertheless, he and Anthia do have a series of misfortunes, typical of the Hellenistic romance, and the dream constitutes a foreshadowing of those misfortunes.

The dreams in Plutarch and in the Hellenistic romances have several features in common with the dream of Cornelius in Acts 10. In each case the dream stands near the beginning of a narrative or an episode within the narrative. The dream does not simply show what will happen but alludes to it in an indirect fashion. In the course of the narrative the dream's meaning becomes clear to the reader, but the dream itself never dominates the narrative. That is, the central characters do not set out to understand the dream.

These similarities mean that Peter's vision need not be viewed as extrinsic to the Cornelius account simply because the vision is not explicitly connected with the larger story. Instead, the vision and the mystery surrounding it *contribute to the drama of the larger narrative.* Since Luke began preparation for this conversion at least as early as Acts 1:8 ("You shall be my witnesses in Jerusalem and in all Judea and Samaria and to the end of the earth"), it is reasonable to conclude that he wishes to make the most of this major event.

If we read the narrative of Cornelius as a continuous whole, we find that it consists of a series of parallel scenes. First, Cornelius sees the divine messenger and then Peter experiences his ecstatic vision. Each receives during his vision a command that is largely unexplained. Second, Cornelius's delegation arrives at Peter's lodging and is welcomed. Likewise, Peter and his colleagues journey to Caesarea and are welcomed by Cornelius. Third, Cornelius makes a brief speech in which he explains why he has summoned Peter. Peter then makes a speech in which he summarizes the Christian kerygma. Finally, the Holy Spirit confirms the rightness of this event by inspiring Cornelius and his household to speak in tongues. Peter then must defend his actions in Jerusalem, where the community also confirms the rightness of the event. This series of parallel scenes may be summarized as follows:

Vision Scene	1	Cornelius	10:1–8
	2	Peter	10:9–16
Journey and Welcome	3	Cornelius	10:17–23a
	4	Peter	10:23b–29

Proclamation	5	Cornelius	10:30–33
	6	Peter	10:34–43
Confirmation	7	Holy Spirit	10:44–48
	8	Community	11:1–18

A closer examination of each of these scenes will show how the repetition in this narrative enhances its dramatic effect. It will also highlight the fact that both Cornelius and Peter require conversion, and it will demonstrate that the abrogation of food laws and the inclusion of Gentiles within the church are inextricably connected.

Scene 1

> At Caesarea there was a man named Cornelius, a centurion of what was known as the Italian Cohort, a devout man who feared God with all his household, gave alms liberally to the people, and prayed constantly to God. About the ninth hour of the day he saw clearly in a vision an angel of God coming in and saying to him, "Cornelius." And he stared at him in terror, and said, "What is it, Lord?" And he said to him, "Your prayers and your alms have ascended as a memorial before God. And now send men to Joppa, and bring one Simon who is called Peter; he is lodging with Simon, a tanner, whose house is by the seaside." When the angel who spoke to him had departed, he called two of his servants and a devout soldier from among those that waited on him, and having related everything to them, he sent them to Joppa. (Acts 10:1–8)

Scene 1, the vision of Cornelius (10:1–8), begins by introducing the reader to Cornelius. He is "a centurion of what was known as the Italian Cohort, a devout man who feared God with all his household, gave alms liberally to the people, and prayed constantly to God" (vv. 1–2). Cornelius is first described as a Gentile, with a responsible position in the Roman army. Because he was in the military, he would have been unable to observe Torah, even had he wished to do so.[40] Nevertheless, Luke leaves no doubt regarding Cornelius's piety. It is appropriate that this centurion become the first Gentile convert.[41]

The angel whom Cornelius sees confirms that Cornelius's piety has been remembered (v. 4b) and then issues an order: "And now send men to Joppa, and bring one Simon who is called Peter; he is lodging with Simon, a tanner, whose house is by the seaside." In one sense this directive is quite full. Cornelius learns where to send his men, which Simon to seek, which Simon is host, and where his house is located. In another sense the directive is extraordinarily brief. The angel says not a single word that indicates what Cornelius or his agents should expect once they have found Simon Peter (cf. Acts 8:26).

One detail of the angel's order is peculiar. He mentions that Simon the tanner has a house by the sea. We might view this as a necessary part of the order, added so that the men will know *where* to look in Joppa. Haenchen comments that tanners lived by the sea because of their work,[42] but if that location was customary, why would Luke bother to mention it? Would not Cornelius's agents—and Luke's audience—know where to find the tanners' section of the city?[43] This detail appears to be superfluous, until we notice how frequently houses and hospitality are mentioned in this narrative. Luke emphasizes the contacts between Cornelius and Peter, especially when those contacts take the form of hospitality, a motif that forms a significant part of Luke's presentation of the Cornelius story.

Scene 2

> The next day, as they were on their journey and coming near the city, Peter went up on the housetop to pray, about the sixth hour. And he became hungry and desired something to eat; but while they were preparing it, he fell into a trance and saw the heaven opened, and something descending, like a great sheet, let down by four corners upon the earth. In it were all kinds of animals and reptiles and birds of the air. And there came a voice to him, "Rise, Peter; kill and eat." But Peter said, "No, Lord; for I have never eaten anything that is common or unclean." And the voice came to him again a second time, "What God has cleansed, you must not call common." This happened three times, and the thing was taken up at once to heaven. (Acts 10:9–16)

Scene 2 connects Peter's vision with what has preceded by noting that it occurred while Cornelius's men were drawing near to Joppa. Peter is engaged in prayer, becomes hungry, and falls into a trance. He sees a vessel in which are "all kinds of animals and reptiles and birds of the air" (v. 12). There follows three times the three-part exchange. A voice orders Peter to rise, kill, and eat. Peter adamantly refuses, saying that he has never eaten anything common or unclean. The voice replies, "What God has cleansed, you must not call common."

Verse 17 indicates that Peter did not understand the vision, and most exegetes would be sympathetic with Peter's confusion. The animals offered to Peter are both clean and unclean, and the fact that they inhabit the same vessel does not alter the distinction. Could not Peter select a clean animal? Does the response of the heavenly voice mean that food laws have been abrogated? If so, why does that abrogation not carry over into the Jerusalem Council in Acts 15? Does the vision refer only to clean and unclean people? If so, why introduce confusion by using food imagery in the vision?

These questions have not found satisfactory resolution.[44] Part of the difficulty may be that exegetes have forgotten that this *is* a vision. To ask why Peter does not choose one of the clean animals is to ignore the ecstatic quality of Peter's experience. The function of the vision is to be suggestive, as is evident in v. 17; it is not intended to portray an actual event. In addition, exegetes have often approached this text by isolating the vision from its context. The resultant expectation is that the meaning of the vision should be clear on its own, although the larger narrative suggests that only later on does Peter understand the vision.

Another problem with conventional readings of Peter's vision stems from an emphasis on the subject matter of the vision (the clean and unclean animals) to the exclusion of the action that occurs within the vision. In the Hebrew Bible, a reference to opening the windows of heaven implies some revelation from God or God's presence (cf. Ps. 78:23; Isa. 24:18; 64:1; Ezek. 1:1). What Peter sees has come from God, and yet the vessel contains all sorts of creatures, clean and unclean! Peter responds to the command emphatically, just as he would have assumed was right and proper. But the heavenly voice does not praise Peter's faithfulness. Neither does the voice reject Peter's faithfulness or comment on it in any way. Instead, the voice says, "What God has cleansed, you must not call common." This pronouncement picks up on the final words of Peter's description, converts them to the appropriate verb forms, and reverses their order:

> Peter: . . . common *(koinon)* and unclean *(akathartos)*
> Voice: What God cleaned *(katharizein)*, do not make common *(koinoun)*

What is at issue between Peter and the voice is not whether Peter eats some particular item for lunch but how he applies the terms "common" and "unclean." His practice is not the subject here, but his assumption that he knows what is clean and what is unclean is! In this sense, the vision may apply to both food and people.[45] More will be clear about that once we have studied the narrative as a whole.

Scene 3

> Now while Peter was inwardly perplexed as to what the vision which he had seen might mean, behold, the men that were sent by Cornelius, having made inquiry for Simon's house, stood before the gate and called out to ask whether Simon who was called Peter was lodging there. And while Peter was pondering the vision, the Spirit said to him, "Behold, three men are looking for you. Rise and go down, and accompany them without hesitation; for I have sent them." And Peter went down to the men and said, "I am the one you are looking for; what is the reason for your coming?" And they said, "Cornelius, a centurion, an upright and God-fearing man, who is well spoken of by the whole Jewish nation, was directed by a holy angel to send for you to come to his house, and to hear what you have to say." So he called them in to be his guests. (Acts 10: 17–23a)

Scene 3 begins by carefully connecting Peter's confusion regarding the vision with the arrival of Cornelius's messengers. Verses 17–18 explain that while Peter was worrying over the vision, Cornelius's men arrive and ask for Simon Peter. Again in vv. 19–20, we read that the dream perplexes Peter, who then hears from the Spirit that three men seek him. Luke underscores the drama of this moment by the use of an intensive form of several key verbs. To be perplexed *(dienthymeomai)*, to make inquiry, to ponder, and to discriminate all have the intensive prefix *dia* in this short passage. When Peter obeys the direction of the Spirit, he learns that these men have been sent to summon him to the house of a Gentile (v. 22). Without further comment he invites them into the house and becomes their host (v. 23; cf. 21:16).

Scene 4

> The next day he rose and went off with them, and some of the brethren from Joppa accompanied him. And on the following day they entered Caesarea. Cornelius was expecting them and had called together his kinsmen and close friends. When Peter entered, Cornelius met him and fell down at his feet and worshiped him. But Peter lifted him up, saying, "Stand up; I too am a man." And as he talked with him, he went in and

found many persons gathered; and he said to them, "You yourselves know how unlawful it is for a Jew to associate with or to visit any one of another nation; but God has shown me that I should not call any man common or unclean. So when I was sent for, I came without objection. I ask then why you sent for me." (Acts 10:23b–29)

Similar elaboration surrounds Peter's arrival at Caesarea in scene 4 (vv. 23b–29). He sets out with Cornelius's men and with some believers from Joppa. When they arrive at Joppa they find Cornelius and all his household waiting for them. Cornelius responds to Peter's arrival by falling at his feet to worship him. Commentators have sometimes read this response as indicating Cornelius's lack of understanding, but that interpretation may itself lack understanding. Cornelius's response to Peter is typical of the welcome a hero receives in the Greek novel (cf. *Ephesian Tale* I, 1.3; 2.7; 12.1) and signifies primarily the respect due to Peter.[46]

Peter raises Cornelius to his feet, and then we read that they enter together and find many who have come. Because both v. 25 and v. 27 describe Peter's entry, questions have arisen. Some explain the repetition of entries as an indication that Luke is bringing together several sources. Others suggest that Peter first enters Cornelius's courtyard and then Cornelius's house. But it is not necessary to explain the repetition as a lapse in Lukan redaction or as slavish realism. As in scene 3, Luke uses the elaborations to draw attention to the coming together of Peter and the Gentiles. That they are together Luke underscores not only with Peter's remarks but also with the repeated use of the prefix *syn* (with) in this scene.[47]

The conclusion of scene 4 recalls that of scene 3. There Cornelius's men summarize Cornelius's experience for Peter. Here in scene 4 Peter summarizes his own: It is unlawful for him to be with them, but God has shown him that he must not call anyone common or unclean. Therefore he has come and asks why he has been summoned.

Scene 5

And Cornelius said, "Four days ago, about this hour, I was keeping the ninth hour of prayer in my house; and behold, a man stood before me in bright apparel, saying, 'Cornelius, your prayer has been heard and your alms have been remembered before God. Send therefore to Joppa and ask for Simon who is called Peter; he is lodging in the house of Simon, a tanner, by the seaside.' So I sent to you at once, and you have been kind enough to come. Now therefore we are all here present in the sight of God, to hear all that you have been commanded by the Lord." (Acts 10:30–33)

Cornelius's response to Peter's question constitutes scene 5. The bulk of his response merely restates his original vision from scene 1. This time, however, Cornelius specifies that he was praying when the messenger appeared,[48] and that the messenger wore "bright apparel" (cf. Luke 24:4; Acts 1:10). The messenger's words vary only slightly from their form in scene 1. Cornelius concludes by announcing solemnly that all are gathered "to hear all that you have been commanded by the Lord" (v. 33; cf. v. 22). Clearly this brief speech has as its primary function the introduction of Peter's sermon. It also reminds the audience that God has initiated this event by means of Cornelius as well as by means of Peter and that Cornelius, whose prayers and alms are remembered, is worthy of what has occurred.

Scene 6

And Peter opened his mouth and said: "Truly I perceive that God shows no partiality, but in every nation any one who fears him and does what is right is acceptable to him. You know the word which he sent to Israel, preaching good news of peace by Jesus Christ (he is Lord of all), the word which was proclaimed throughout all Judea, beginning from Galilee after the baptism which John preached: how God anointed Jesus of Nazareth with the Holy Spirit and with power; how he went about doing good and healing all that were oppressed by the devil, for God was with him. And we are witnesses to all that he did both in the country of the Jews and in Jerusalem. They put him to death by hanging him on a tree; but God raised him on the third day and made him manifest; not to all the people but to us who were chosen by God as witnesses, who ate and drank with him after he rose from the dead. And he commanded us to preach to the people, and to testify that he is the one ordained by God to be judge of the living and the dead. To him all the prophets bear witness that every one who believes in him receives forgiveness of sins through his name." (Acts 10:34–43)

Like Cornelius's speech, much of Peter's speech in scene 6 recapitulates earlier material. Here the material repeated comes from earlier speeches in Acts rather than from within this particular narrative. That is, the bulk of Peter's speech recollects earlier speeches of Peter (2:17–36; 3:12–26) and Paul's later speech at Antioch (13:26–41).

There are, however, several ways in which Luke has adapted this speech to its context.[49]

The introduction to the speech explicitly reflects the context (cf. 2:14–15; 3:12). What Peter says in v. 34, that there is no partiality with God, can be found also in the Hebrew Bible and in deutero-canonical literature, where the context of God's impartiality is assumed to be Israel (e.g., Deut. 10:17; 2 Chron. 19:7; Sir. 35:12–13). Here, however, Peter declares what he has learned: Anyone who fears God (cf. 10:2, 22) and behaves accordingly is acceptable.

This pronouncement does not simply link the speech to its context. This is Peter's third statement concerning the events that are occurring, and here for the first time he seems to have grasped the significance of his summons to Caesarea. When Cornelius's messengers arrived at Joppa (v. 21), Peter responded in an uncommitted manner: "I am the one you are looking for" (v. 21). Upon entering Cornelius's home, Peter said that such commerce with Gentiles was unlawful, yet "God has shown me that I should not call any man common or unclean" (v. 28). Following Cornelius's explanation of why he sent for Peter, Peter recognizes that even more has been established: There is no partiality! The full implications of this insight for the Christian community have yet to be worked out, but here God's decision is acknowledged by the leader of the Jerusalem church.

A further indication of the contextualization of Peter's speech comes in v. 36, when Peter interjects the exclamation: "He is lord of all." This comment is sufficiently awkward in the Greek that most translators place it in parentheses. The material surrounding this parenthesis conforms to the content of Peter's earlier speeches, but the conclusion that Jesus is indeed lord of *all* people appears here in a new and more explicit way than has been the case earlier (cf. 2:39).[50]

Another way in which Luke seems to have tailored this speech to its setting is that he dwells on the life of Jesus in more detail than is the case in the earlier speeches.[51] And yet v. 36, which inaugurates the sketch of Jesus' life, says "you know" what has occurred. Some scholars see this as an indication that the speech does not fit its context at all because Cornelius and company do *not* know the events surrounding Jesus' life. Wilckens has suggested that "you know" is intended for Luke's audience rather than for Cornelius.[52] Another possibility is that the "you know" is a polite gesture, one that respects

Cornelius as representative of Rome and suggests to the reader that the events of Jesus' life were broadly known (cf. 26:26).

Most of what Peter says about Jesus' life expands material in the earlier speeches only slightly. For example, Peter goes into some detail regarding the healings done by Jesus (cf. 2:22). One of these expansions seems curiously appropriate to the Cornelius episode. In v. 41 Peter specifies that the witnesses include those whom God chose, those "who ate and drank with him after he rose from the dead." None of the other speeches in Acts refer to this qualification of the witnesses, but it is especially appropriate for a story that concerns itself with hospitality for Gentiles. Note that Peter's critics in Jerusalem focus on this particular act (Acts 11:3).

Peter's sermon moves toward its customary conclusion by announcing that all who believe in Jesus will receive forgiveness of sins (cf. 2:38–39; 3:19–20). He does not, however, promise the gift of the Holy Spirit, for Peter himself is now to be interrupted by the Spirit.

Scene 7

> While Peter was still saying this, the Holy Spirit fell on all who heard the word. And the believers from among the circumcised who came with Peter were amazed, because the gift of the Holy Spirit had been poured out even on the Gentiles. For they heard them speaking in tongues and extolling God. Then Peter declared, "Can any one forbid water for baptizing these people who have received the Holy Spirit just as we have?" And he commanded them to be baptized in the name of Jesus Christ. Then they asked him to remain for some days. (Acts 10:44–48)

We might expect to find in scene 7 some response to Peter's sermon, but Cornelius and his household neither profess belief nor ask what is required of them. Instead, even while Peter is speaking, the Holy Spirit falls on all (v. 44). Nowhere else does the Spirit come before baptism. Such an unprecedented gift causes the believers who are with Peter to respond as to a miracle—with amazement. Peter himself responds that these Gentiles cannot be denied baptism and, subsequently, he orders that baptism. Although commentators sometimes dwell on Peter's action as an indication of his apostolic authority, something else is at work here. Just as Peter has been the one throughout the narrative who announced the importance of events (vv. 21, 28, 34–35), so also now he announces their full implication.

Gentiles cannot be denied baptism because God has overtly and unmistakably included them.

The closing remark in scene 7 deserves comment. Luke adds this notice: "Then they asked him to remain for some days" (v. 48b). Consistent with the entire narrative, this request suggests that the inclusion of Gentiles does not have to do merely with a grudging admission to the circle of the baptized. Including Gentiles means receiving them, entering their homes, and accepting hospitality in those homes.[53]

Scene 8

Now the apostles and the brethren who were in Judea heard that the Gentiles also had received the word of God. So when Peter went up to Jerusalem, the circumcision party criticized him, saying, "Why did you go to uncircumcised men and eat with them?" But Peter began and explained to them in order: "I was in the city of Joppa praying and in a trance I saw a vision, something descending, like a great sheet, let down from heaven by four corners; and it came down to me. Looking at it closely I observed animals and beasts of prey and reptiles and birds of the air. And I heard a voice saying to me, 'Rise, Peter; kill and eat.' But I said, 'No, Lord; for nothing common or unclean has ever entered my mouth.' But the voice answered a second time from heaven, 'What God has cleansed you must not call common.' This happened three times, and all was drawn up again into heaven. At that very moment three men arrived at the house in which we were, sent to me from Caesarea. And the Spirit told me to go with them, making no distinction. These six brethren also accompanied me, and we entered the man's house. And he told us how he had seen the angel standing in his house and saying, 'Send to Joppa and bring Simon called Peter; he will declare to you a message by which you will be saved, you and all your household.' As I began to speak, the Holy Spirit fell on them just as on us at the beginning. And I remembered the word of the Lord, how he said, 'John baptized with water, but you shall be baptized with the Holy Spirit.' If then God gave the same gift to them as he gave to us when we believed in the Lord Jesus Christ, who was I that I could withstand God?" When they heard this they were silenced. And they glorified God, saying, "Then to the Gentiles also God has granted repentance unto life." (Acts 11:1–18)

At first glance 11:1–18 seems disproportionately long to be regarded as one scene in this highly developed story. Nevertheless, 11:1–18 has one main point, the confirmation of the community. Its length derives from the fact that it repeats much of what has already occurred.

As the scene opens believers in Jerusalem hear that the Gentiles have received the word of God (11:1), and those of the circumcision party respond critically to Peter. They charge him with going to uncircumcised men and eating with them (11:2). Haenchen regards Luke as having softened the Jerusalem reaction to Peter. Because Luke does not wish to acknowledge that some rejected the inclusion of Gentiles, he substitutes the lesser complaint concerning Peter's table-fellowship.[54] But this interpretation fails to see the pervasive thread of hospitality that runs throughout this narrative. It also overlooks the fact that the inclusion of Gentiles and table-fellowship with Gentiles are inseparably related. To balk at eating with Gentiles is to balk at receiving them into the community.

Within the narrative, the function of the accusation is to allow Peter (and Luke) to review the events leading up to his disputed table-fellowship. Although Peter relates the story from his perspective (thus beginning with his own vision) and in first person, much of what Peter says is a word-for-word repetition of Acts 10.

The major change within the review of events occurs in v. 14. In earlier versions, Cornelius's visitor merely directs him to summon Peter (10:5-6, 32). The most that is said is when Cornelius's messengers explain to Peter that Cornelius has been told that he will "hear words" from Peter (10:22). Now, however, we learn that Cornelius expects Peter to present a message of salvation for Cornelius and his household (11:14). What follows immediately is the gift of the Holy Spirit, which confirms that this is indeed a message of salvation.[55]

Peter declares to his challengers that the coming of the Spirit to these Gentiles reminded him of Jesus' promise of a Spirit-baptism. Since the Gentiles have received the same gift as other believers, Peter asks, "Who was I that I could withstand God?" Peter's question forces the issue. His challengers are silenced. The scene and the larger narrative conclude with their response. They glorify God because God has granted "repentance unto life" even to the Gentiles.

Whatever tradition Luke may have received regarding the conversion of the first Gentile, he has woven it here into one dramatic and effective narrative. He employs repetition in order to make his point clear, and yet he is able to sustain interest by revealing certain aspects of the story only gradually (e.g., Peter's response, the content of the words Peter is to speak, the eventual table-fellowship between Peter and Cornelius and their respective companions). The visions of the main characters and their responses to them Luke intertwines in a particularly effective manner. A number of elements in the narrative recall elements in the conversion of the Ethiopian eunuch and the conversion of Saul, but they appear here in a yet more pronounced way.

The conclusion to which Luke points is unmistakable: God has included the Gentiles, and the church may not resist. The implications of that decision become clearer in the following chapters of Acts. Not only is the decision unmistakable, but it forms the climax of the first half of Acts, with 11:19–15:35 forming the denouement.[56] Immediately following the Cornelius narrative, we read of the formation of a Gentile Christian community in Antioch (11:19–26). With the beginning of the mission of Paul and Barnabas begins also the pattern of rejection by the synagogue and acceptance by Gentiles (13:44–52). Finally in Acts 15 it becomes necessary that the Jerusalem leaders address directly the events that already have occurred.

The significance of the Cornelius narrative for the larger narrative of Acts is obvious, but what does the story indicate regarding Cornelius as a convert? Here the answer is quite similar to what we have found elsewhere in Acts. Luke shows little interest in explaining the conversion itself, Cornelius's change of mind. We hear no confession of faith or request for baptism. Cornelius's conversion is so completely controlled by God that Cornelius himself remains quite passive. Luke thus does not present Cornelius as a typical or exemplary convert, but as a symbolic or representative one.

Indeed, we could ask whether this is a conversion. Given the typology I suggested in my introductions, Cornelius appears to undergo alternation rather than conversion. While his is a significant change, Luke takes great care to explain that Cornelius is already a pious, devout follower of God. There is no rejection of the past required here, nor is Cornelius in need of a transformed view of the world.

CONCLUSION

Because Luke's narrative garment is rich and complex, it is difficult to turn from a description of certain parts of the garment in order to take up a more comprehensive analysis. As we pull together what we have learned here, we look first at the function of Acts 8—10 and then at the common threads in Luke's treatment of conversion.

The Acts of the Apostles contains stories about the conversion of three individuals. These stories are arranged in such a way that they follow one another in very close order, leaving aside for the moment the subsequent retellings of Paul's conversion. Given the care with which Luke writes, it is improbable that the order is merely accidental. Luke has placed the three together so that he can dramatically present the fulfillment of Acts 1:8. With the completion of Acts 10 (or 11:1–18), the gospel has reached the "end of the earth."

The Ethiopian eunuch begins the series. Coming from what Luke's audience would have regarded as the other end of the world, the eunuch is a mysterious, even exotic, personage. He has status and prestige, and his interest in Jerusalem makes him a sympathetic figure. Beginning and ending in an odd way, his conversion is a joyous event, controlled entirely by the Holy Spirit. For Luke, he is neither the first Gentile convert *nor* a proselyte to Judaism. Instead, he symbolizes all those from earth's end who, unlike Jerusalem Jews, *will* receive the gospel. Indeed, the Ethiopian does not merely receive the gospel but reaches out to grasp it.

Immediately following the story of the eunuch comes that of Saul. The two episodes have certain similarities, in that God or the Spirit directs each episode, each occurs during travel, and each involves a mediator (Philip, Ananias). The dissimilar features are more significant, however. Saul is not, to say the least, a willing hearer of the good news. And Ananias does not silently acquiesce to the strange command he receives about Saul (contrast Philip in Acts 8:27). These dissimilarities arise from the fact that Luke insists in countless ways on Saul's identity as *enemy* of the church. Unlike either the Ethiopian or Cornelius, Saul is a Jew, but his behavior as enemy has removed him from those who may legitimately be called "brother." He appears in Acts 7 and again at the beginning of Acts 9 as *the* enemy of the church. Unlike other enemies (cf. 12:20–23), he is not killed but converted. The gospel has power even over its enemies.

After the story of Saul's initial proclamation of the gospel, Luke inserts two brief stories, the healing of Aeneas (9:32–35) and the raising of Dorcas from the dead (9:36–43). Each story concludes with a notice that many people "believed in the Lord" or "turned to the Lord." Following these stories, which reintroduce Peter, Luke tells the story of Cornelius and Peter.

Here again there are elements reminiscent of the eunuch and of Saul. The double vision of Ananias and Saul reappears in a more developed way in the double vision of Peter and Cornelius. Once again, a representative of the church is sent in the form of Peter, who protests against the task (10:9–16; cf. Ananias in 9:10–16). The series of conversions culminates here. If the inclusion of the eunuch symbolized the beginning of the gospel's movement to the end of the earth, the inclusion of Cornelius makes of that symbol an explicit fact. Not only is the first Gentile converted, but Peter, as representative of the church, is also converted in that he finally sees that he has no right to determine what God has cleansed and what God has not cleansed.

At the beginning of Acts 8, the Jerusalem church has experienced the devastation of Stephen's death and the concomitant end of its growth. The scattering of believers outside Jerusalem seems to signal the death of the community. Of course, the story is not over but just beginning, and that is the point Luke makes with force in the conversion stories of Acts 8—10.

What do these stories and others reveal about Luke's understanding of conversion? Certainly Luke does not present in any of these stories an ideal or typical account of conversion. Each individual whose conversion appears in Acts represents some larger group or some thread in Luke's narrative. No conversion, not even that of the crowd at Pentecost, establishes a pattern that is followed by later believers or is appealed to in preaching.

Related to this is the fact that, for Luke, a conversion story is not an end in itself. He tells *about* the conversions of groups and of individuals, but he is not interested in conversion stories per se. The conversions Luke includes all appear in connection with some larger issue in the community's development.

As is the case with much else in Luke–Acts, conversion is a gift from God. God directly initiates all of the individual conversions that take place, and extraordinary events brought about by God stand behind some of the mass conversions (e.g., 2:1–13; 3:1–10). The leadership of the community can take little credit. Although Philip seems ready enough to comply with orders, he takes little initiative with the eunuch. Ananias and Peter almost have to be dragged kicking and screaming. Conversion comes from God.

The fact that we have focused on stories about individual converts should not be misread. These are not private or individualistic experiences. The mass conversions end in the fellowship of worship and bread (2:43–47). As isolated as Paul is when he is reduced to blindness, his conversion is complete only when Ananias, the church's representative, finally does accept him and when Barnabas introduces him at Jerusalem. Central to the story of Peter and Cornelius is the community's acceptance of Cornelius *and* of Peter's action. Even the eunuch, who goes "on his way rejoicing," has connections through Philip with the larger fellowship.

For Luke, stories of conversion are stories about beginnings—the beginning of the Jerusalem community, the beginning of the church in Samaria and beyond, the beginning of triumph over the church's enemies. Conversion also begins the response of an individual to a calling (9:15–16) and the response of a community to its calling (11:1–18). Conversion can only be described as part of the Lukan garment.

NOTES

1. On the infancy narratives, see R. E. Brown, *The Birth of the Messiah* (Garden City, N.Y.: Doubleday & Co., 1977).

2. E.g., Hans Conzelmann, *Theology of St. Luke,* trans. G. Buswell (Philadelphia: Fortress Press, 1982 [1953]), 99–101.

3. See above, 41–43.

4. Haenchen acknowledges that Luke has no "systematic teaching" on conversion, but he then derives from a number of scenes the "essential" steps in conversion (*Acts,* 94). Ulrich Wilckens sees in Acts 2:38 an *ordo salutis* (*Die Missionsreden des Apostelgeschichte,* WMANT 15 [Neukirchen-Vluyn: Neukirchener-Verlag, 1963], 178–86).

5. James Crampsey laments the fact that Luke's *idea* of conversion has been discussed, but individual stories have not received attention in that

discussion (*The Conversion of Cornelius* [*10:1—11:18*]: *Societal Apologetic and Ecclesial Tension* [Ann Arbor, Mich.: University Microfilms, 1983], 1–2).

6. Notice that the church does not plan and organize its first mission outside Jerusalem. Instead, the church is pushed into action. See Beverly Roberts Gaventa, " 'You Will Be My Witnesses': Aspects of Mission in the Acts of the Apostles," *Missiology* 10 (1982): 27–42.

7. The story of Peter and Simon (Acts 8:9–24) is not a conversion story but a story of confrontation between the gospel and magic.

8. Eusebius, *Hist. eccl.* 2.2.13–14. Irenaeus also says that the eunuch was "sent into the regions of Ethiopia, to preach what he had himself believed" (*Adv. Haer.* 3.12.8).

9. Adolf von Harnack, *Beitrage zur Einleitung in das Neue Testament*, 7 vols. (Leipzig: J. C. Hinrichs, 1908), 3:150–51.

10. Martin Dibelius, *Studies in the Acts of the Apostles*, trans. Mary Ling (London: SCM Press; New York: Charles Scribner's Sons, 1956), 15.

11. Dibelius, *Acts*, 315–16.

12. van Unnik, "Philippus," 328–29.

13. Kirsopp Lake and Henry Cadbury, *The Beginnings of Christianity*, 4 vols. (London: Macmillan & Co., 1920–33), 4:95; F. F. Bruce, *The Acts of the Apostles*, 2d ed. (Grand Rapids: Wm. B. Eerdmans, 1952), 190; Haenchen, *Acts*, 310–11. Erich Dinkler argues that the movement south helps to fulfill Acts 1:8, just as chapter 10 describes the westward mission ("Philippus und der *anēr aithiops* [Apg. 8.26–40]: Historische und geographische Bemerkungen zum Missionsablauf nach Lukas," *Jesus und Paulus*, ed. E. E. Ellis and Erich Grässer [Göttingen: Vandenhoeck & Ruprecht, 1975], 86–87).

14. van Unnik, "Philippus," 328–39.

15. Here the RSV has resolved another ambiguity in the Greek, where the adjective "desert" or "desolate" may refer either to the road or to the city of Gaza. Given the fact that the encounter between the two occurs on the road rather than in the city, it appears that Luke is describing the road rather than the city. So it is taken by many: A. T. Robertson, *A Grammar of the Greek New Testament in the Light of Historical Research*, 2d ed. (London: Hodder & Stoughton, 1914), 698; Dibelius, *Acts*, 15; BAGD, 149; BDF, 151; Turner, *Syntax*, 44; van Unnik, "Philippus," 329–30.

16. van Unnik, "Philippus," 335–37.

17. Both the directions of the angel and Philip's response recall similar commissionings in the Septuagint. See 1 Kings 17:8–10; Ezek. 3:22–23; Jonah 1:1–3; 3:1–3.

18. Haenchen, *Acts*, 316.

19. See above, 94, n. 19.

20. F. M. Snowden, Jr., "Early Christianity and Blacks," *IDBSup*, 111; *Oxford Classical Dictionary*, ed. N. G. L. Hammond and H. H. Scullard, 2d

ed. (Oxford: At the Clarendon Press, 1970), 408–9. Numerous texts are cited.

21. See, for example, Homer, *Odyssey* 1.22–24; Aeschylus, *Suppliants* 284–86; Herodotus 3.17–23; 7.69–70; Diodorus Siculus 3.1–37; Strabo 17.2.1–3; Pliny 6.35; Dio Cassius 54.5.4.

22. For a detailed examination of these issues see F. M. Snowden, Jr., *Blacks in Antiquity* (Cambridge: Harvard Univ. Press, 1970); idem, *Before Color Prejudice* (Cambridge: Harvard Univ. Press, 1983).

23. Pliny, *Natural History* 6.35.186; H. J. Cadbury, *The Book of Acts in History* (New York: Harper & Brothers, 1955), 16–17; E. A. Budge, *A History of Ethiopia*, 2 vols. (Oosterhout N.B.: Anthropological Publications, 1970 [1928]), 111–13.

24. Dio Cassius 54.5.4; Strabo 17.1.54; Pliny 6.35; Dinkler, "Philippus," 91.

25. Seneca, *Nat. Quaest.* 6.8.3; Tacitus, *Annales* 15; Dio Cassius 68:8.1; Dinkler, "Philippus," 91.

26. Dinkler, "Philippus," 92.

27. Josephus, *Antiquities* 3.318, *War* 4.275; Suetonius, *Divus Augustus* 93. Emil Schürer, *The History of the Jewish People in the Age of Jesus Christ*, 2 vols., rev. and ed. G. Vermes, F. Millar, and M. Black (Edinburgh: T. & T. Clark, 1979), 2:309–13.

28. Ronald Hock has demonstrated that reading was a customary way of employing travel time in antiquity (*The Social Context of Paul's Ministry: Tentmaking and Apostleship* [Philadelphia: Fortress Press, 1980], 28).

29. The Greek contains a word play *(ginōskeis ha anaginōskeis)* that is maintained in the Vulgate *(intelligis quae legis)* but lost in English translations.

30. Haenchen, *Acts*, 311.

31. Given the frequent allusions to Isaiah 53 in the New Testament and Luke's own interest in Isaiah, this choice is not surprising. It is, nevertheless, the first time that Luke has explicitly related a passage from Isaiah 53 to the death of Jesus.

32. Bruce, *Acts*, 194.

33. Dibelius, "The Conversion of Cornelius," 109–22. Conzelmann concurs with this analysis (*Die Apostlegeschichte*, HNT, 2d ed. [Tübingen: J. C. B. Mohr (Paul Siebeck), 1972], 69).

34. Haenchen, *Acts*, 360–63.

35. Ulrich Wilckens, "Kerygma und Evangelium bei Lukas (Beobachtungen zu Acta 10:34–43)," *ZNW* 49 (1958): 223–37.

36. Francois Bovon, "Tradition et redaction en Actes 10,1–11,18," *Theologische Zeitschrift* 26 (1970): 22–45.

37. Karl Löning, "Die Korneliustradition," *BZ* 18 (1974): 1–19.

38. Klaus Haacker, "Dibelius und Cornelius: Ein Beispiel formgeschichtlicher Überlieferungskritik," *BZ* 24 (1980): 234–51.

39. Alfred Wikenhauser, "Doppetraüme," *Biblica* 29 (1948): 110–111. To Wikenhauser's list may be added Achilles Tatius, *Leucippe and Clitophon* 4:1 and Longus, *Daphnis and Chloe* 1:78.

40. Josephus, *Antiquities* 18.84. See also W. C. van Unnik, "The Background and Significance of Acts x.4 and 35," in *Sparsa Collecta*, 1:249.

41. Haenchen concludes from Cornelius that Luke is arguing that the church accepted only Gentiles of true piety (*Acts*, 357–58). However acceptable Cornelius's actions may be, they do not figure prominently in the story. Cornelius's virtues explain why he is the first Gentile convert, not how others may seek conversion.

42. Ibid., 347.

43. Ramsay MacMullen, *Roman Social Relations* (New Haven: Yale Univ. Press, 1974), 71–73; Hock, *Social Context*, 32.

44. See Haenchen, *Acts*, 358, 361–63, for a survey of various interpretations.

45. Attempts to distinguish between the abrogation of food laws and the inclusion of Gentiles are in any case unconvincing. Food laws became an issue not because Jewish Christians desired to eat pork, but because Gentiles were attracted to the Christian faith. Any broad movement of Gentiles into the Christian community necessitated an examination of this issue.

46. Contrast this welcome with the clear misunderstanding of the people of Lystra who explicitly call Paul and Barnabas gods (14:11–13). For *The Ephesian Tale*, see M. Hadas, *Three Greek Romances* (Indianapolis: Bobbs Merrill, 1964).

47. *Synerxesthai* (v. 23, v. 27), *syngkalien* (v. 24), *syggeneis* (v. 24), *synantan* (v. 25), and *synomilein* (v. 27).

48. What Peter says, translated literally, is that he has been praying continually for four days. Haenchen takes this to be the result of a copyist's error (*Acts*, 350).

49. Dibelius argues that Luke has fit this speech to its context only in the introduction (vv. 35–36) ("Conversion of Cornelius," 111). Wilson, however, concludes that Luke "constructed the speech with one eye on the context and the other on the stereotyped pattern of the speeches in the early part of Acts" (*The Gentiles and the Gentile Mission in Luke-Acts*, 175). Haacker comes to a similar conclusion ("Dibelius und Cornelius," 241–45).

50. Haacker, "Dibelius und Cornelius," 245.

51. Ibid. Also Wilckens, "Kerygma und Evangelium bei Lukas," 226–29.

52. Ibid., 226.

53. *Epimenein*, translated "to remain" in the RSV, appears later in the accounts of hospitality extended to Paul. See Acts 21:4; 28:12, 14. See also Abraham J. Malherbe, "Hospitality and Inhospitality in the Church," in *Social Aspects of Early Christianity*, 2d ed., enl. (Philadelphia: Fortress Press 1983 [1977]), 92–112.

54. Haenchen, *Acts*, 354, 359.

55. Commentators often worry that 11:15 ("As I began to speak . . .") contradicts Acts 10, where the Holy Spirit interrupts Peter only after he has been speaking for some time. By comparison with earlier speeches in Acts (Peter's Pentecost speech and Stephen's defense), Peter's brief remarks in Acts 10 would seem to be a mere beginning. In addition, Peter's review is intended to move quickly to demonstrate that his action was inevitable, not to repeat the kerygma for believers!

56. Similarly, Paul's final defense speech is the climax of the second half of Acts, with the trip to Rome and events there forming the denouement of that story.

CHAPTER 4

"By His Great Mercy
We Have Been Born Anew"

Imagery of New Birth and New Life

For those who are accustomed to contemporary Christian discussion about being "born again," the virtual absence of this motif in the New Testament may come as a surprise. Conversion as new birth or new life, which is not the equivalent of "born again," is far from being a dominant motif in the New Testament. On the contrary, imagery of new birth appears primarily in the literature of the Johannine community and in 1 Peter.[1] In each of those contexts the motif of new birth is significant because it brings together some central elements in the writer's understanding of faith. Thus, while language of new birth is not plentiful in the New Testament, it does play an important role in introducing us to a distinct perspective on the Christian community.

Just as language of birth and new life appears less often than some might expect, it also has a character that some will find surprising. In contemporary usage, to be "born again" refers most often to the experience of an individual. The outcome of that experience is an intense personal relationship of the individual with Jesus. While it may be assumed that the "born again" Christian becomes a member of a church, little emphasis is placed on the role of Christian community and less on any ethical component of faith. We will see that the use of language of new life and birth from above in the New Testament is not confined to the realm of personal experience.

Perhaps the first thing to be noted is that concepts of new birth and new life are not original in or unique to early Christianity. Already in postexilic Judaism there are references to being or becoming God's children (Wisd. of Sol. 2:13, 16, 18; 5:5; Sir. 4:10; 23:1, 4).[2] Philo speaks of the soul's life *(paliggenesia)* after death (*On the Cherubim* 114) and Josephus of the rebirth of the ashes of Sodom (*War* 4.484). Later on, the proselyte is described in the Talmud as "a child just born" (b. Yebam. 22a).

Images of new birth also appear outside of Judaism. In the second-century work *Metamorphoses,* Apuleius narrates the unfortunate story of Lucius, whose interest in magic turns him into a donkey, and who receives a new life by the grace of Isis (11.22). In the Hermetic corpus, Poimandres offers instruction on how humans may escape their bodies into true life (1,24) or rebirth (13,16).

Given the geographical and chronological distribution of these references, it is impossible to discern the origin and development of this imagery of birth and renewal. What we have is a conventional way of referring to conversion or renewal. As we turn to the major uses of this imagery in the New Testament, then, the question we need to ask is how the imagery is understood and employed.

THE JOHANNINE LITERATURE

> Now there was a man of the Pharisees, named Nicodemus, a ruler of the Jews. This man came to Jesus by night and said to him, "Rabbi, we know that you are a teacher come from God; for no one can do these signs that you do, unless God is with him." Jesus answered him, "Truly, truly, I say to you, unless one is born anew, he cannot see the kingdom of God." Nicodemus said to him, "How can a man be born when he is old? Can he enter a second time into his mother's womb and be born?" Jesus answered, "Truly, truly, I say to you, unless one is born of water and the Spirit, he cannot enter the kingdom of God. That which is born of the flesh is flesh, and that which is born of the Spirit is spirit. Do not marvel that I said to you, 'You must be born anew.' The wind blows where it wills, and you hear the sound of it, but you do not know whence it comes or whither it goes; so it is with every one who is born of the Spirit." Nicodemus said to him, "How can this be?" Jesus answered him, "Are you a teacher of Israel, and yet you do not understand this? Truly, truly, I say to you, we speak of what we know, and bear witness to what we have seen; but you do not receive our testimony. If I have told you earthly things and you do not believe, how can you believe if I tell you heavenly things? No one has ascended into heaven but he who descended from heaven, the Son of man. And as Moses lifted up the serpent in the wilderness, so must the Son of man be lifted up, that whoever believes in him may have eternal life." (John 3:1–15)

The meeting between Jesus and Nicodemus opens in an intriguing way. The narrator has just explained that many believed in Jesus' name because of his signs, but Jesus himself did *not* believe the people because he knew them and needed no testimony about them (John 2:23–25). The RSV obscures the fact that the same verb, *pisteuein* (to believe, to trust), is used both of the people's attitude toward Jesus and of Jesus' attitude toward those around him. It is from this complex background of trust and the lack thereof that Nicodemus emerges.

John's description of Nicodemus raises more questions than answers. Nicodemus is a Pharisee and a ruler of the Jews. He approaches Jesus at night, not with a question but with an assertion that Jesus is indeed a teacher sent from God. As is frequently the case in John, Jesus' response to Nicodemus leaves Nicodemus confused, and Nicodemus's confusion in turn gives Jesus an opportunity for elaboration. In the ensuing discourse (3:11–21) Nicodemus quickly fades from view.

How are we to understand the character Nicodemus and his approach to Jesus? The fact that he is said to be a leader of the Jews causes some to think that Nicodemus is a "representative of the old order which is being superseded."[3] But Nicodemus does come to Jesus in search of some understanding, and he has clearly been impressed by Jesus.[4] Furthermore, his later appearances in the Gospel should prevent us from seeing Nicodemus as a mere stick-figure who stands in for Jesus' Jewish opponents:

> The officers then went back to the chief priests and Pharisees, who said to them, "Why did you not bring him?" The officers answered, "No man ever spoke like this man!" The Pharisees answered, "Are you led astray, you also! Have any of the authorities or of the Pharisees believed in him? But this crowd, who do not know the law, is accursed." *Nicodemus, who had gone to him before, and who was one of them, said to them, "Does our law judge a man without first giving him a hearing and learning what he does?"* They replied, "Are you from Galilee too? Search and you will see that no prophet is to rise from Galilee: (John 7:45–52, italics mine)

Here Nicodemus occupies a volatile middle ground. John describes him as having gone to Jesus earlier *and* as being "one of them." That the description is a contradiction in terms becomes clear when Nicodemus's question about just procedure meets with a sharp and conclusive answer.

Nicodemus appears one more time in the Gospel, following the crucifixion:

> After this Joseph of Arimathea, who was a disciple of Jesus, but secretly, for fear of the Jews . . . came and took away his body. *Nicodemus also, who had first come to him by night,* came bringing a mixture of myrrh and aloes, about a hundred pounds' weight. (John 19:38–39, italics mine)

Nicodemus's association with Joseph of Arimathea in this incident suggests that, like Joseph, he has come to believe but has feared to make his faith public (12:42).[5] John may well use both Nicodemus and Joseph of Arimathea to invite secret believers in his own community to make their faith known and to come out from the synagogue.[6]

When Nicodemus first enters the narrative, then, John carefully connects him with the Jewish community and its "official" attitude toward Jesus. He comes to Jesus at night, a time John associates elsewhere with the realm of unbelief and falsehood (9:4; 11:10; 13:30). His initial comment to Jesus is not a question, as it is often taken, but a statement about how Jesus is perceived by the leadership: "Rabbi, we know that you are a teacher come from God; for no one can do these signs that you do, unless God is with him" (3:2).

Nicodemus, a leader of the people, approves of Jesus. He understands Jesus to be a teacher, a title Jesus receives gladly elsewhere in the Gospel (1:38; 11:28; 13:13–14; 20:16). Like those who are mentioned at the end of John 2, Nicodemus responds to the signs of Jesus. And Jesus, consistent with what is said about him in John 2, does not trust the statement of Nicodemus. Instead, he responds to Nicodemus with a baffling pronouncement that opens the way for his discourse: "Truly, truly, I say to you, unless one is born anew *(gennēthē anōthen)* he cannot see the kingdom of God (3:3)."

So the RSV translates, necessarily choosing one of several meanings for the Greek word *anōthen* and thereby obscuring the double entendre that is essential for understanding the passage. What Jesus says is that one must be born *anōthen,* but *anōthen* can mean either "from above" as in

> Every good endowment and every perfect gift is *from above,* coming down from the Father of lights with whom there is no variation or shadow due to change. (James 1:17; cf. James 3:15)

Or *anōthen* can mean "again" as in

> How can you turn back again to the weak and beggarly elemental spirits, whose slaves you want to be *once more*?[7] (Gal. 4:9; Josephus, *Ant.* 1.263)

Nicodemus hears Jesus' statement as if the,latter use of *anōthen* had been intended and responds with the logical question, "How can a man be born when he is old?" His interpretation of Jesus' question does not arise from some moral or intellectual flaw. Nicodemus simply hears the words of Jesus on an "earthly" level, to enter a second time (*deuteron eiselthein*, v.4), when they are supposed to be heard spiritually.

A similar misunderstanding, arising from double meaning, occurs during Jesus' encounter with the Samaritan woman. Upon hearing Jesus' offer of *zōn* water (John 4:7–15), the woman concludes that he knows where *running* water may be located, while Jesus intends to offer *living* or spiritual water. Many of Jesus' sayings in John involve a double meaning, with the result that ironic misunderstanding appears throughout the gospel.[8] The irony continues in contemporary Christianity, since the meaning of *anōthen* that Jesus rejects has become a dominant way of describing conversion.

That, for the Johannine Jesus, *anōthen* means "from above" is clear when we examine its appearance in 3:31 ("He who comes from above [*anōthen*] is above all . . .") and in 19:11 ("You would have no power over me unless it had been given you from above [*anōthen*] . . ."). As Jesus is "from above" so his followers are born "from above."

In vv. 5–8, when Jesus explains to Nicodemus what he means, it becomes clear that what is required is a spiritual birth:

> Truly, truly, I say to you, unless one is born of water and of the spirit, he cannot enter the kingdom of God. That which is born of the flesh is flesh, and that which is born of the Spirit is spirit. Do not marvel that I said to you, "You must be born anew" (*gennēthēnai anōthen*). The wind blows (*hopou*) where it wills, and you hear the sound of it, but you do not know whence (*pothen*) it comes or whither (*pou*) it goes; so it is with every one who is born of the spirit.

Being born *anōthen* is birth "of water and of spirit" or, more literally, "of water and spirit." Since water does not reappear in the discussion, it is difficult to understand exactly what is intended here. Certainly "of water" refers to baptism,[9] but the relationship between water and spirit is left unexplained. Does baptism provide the occasion for the reception of the Spirit? Are these two events separate but equally necessary? We are given no clues for answering those questions, and can only conclude that the evangelist is not interested in the formal relationship between baptism and the Spirit, but sees the necessity of each.[10]

In what follows, attention focuses on birth "of spirit." Verse 6 suggests a sharp dichotomy between flesh and spirit. What is born of the spirit *is* spirit or belongs to the spirit. Employing the word *pneuma,* which means both wind and spirit, John compares the activity of the wind with that of the Spirit. Neither can be controlled or directed, but each acts of its own accord (cf. Eccles. 11:5; Sir. 16:21). When Nicodemus still does not understand Jesus' words, Jesus asks how Nicodemus can be a teacher of Israel and fail to understand. (Of course, in John's Gospel, nearly everyone fails to understand.) The remainder of the discourse (vv. 11–21) turns from spiritual rebirth to the relationship between Jesus and God.

In order to understand more fully these terse sayings about being born "from above" or born "of water and spirit," we need to read them in light of the larger Johannine context. At least three aspects of this spiritual birth need to be noted and elucidated: discontinuity, relationship to Jesus, and reception of a new spirit.

To cast the requirements for entry into God's kingdom into the language of birth is, first, a radical move that assumes there is discontinuity in the life of the one so born. The use of birth imagery is not radical because it is unique to Christians,[11] but because of the inherent radicality of suggesting that human beings can experience a new birth or a different kind of birth. What is involved here is not an improvement of the individual, but a new origin for the individual.[12] The old origin in flesh and the new origin in Spirit are discontinuous with one another. Elsewhere in John's Gospel this discontinuity is conveyed by the distinction between this world and that above (8:23–24; 15:18–19) and by imagery of light or sight and darkness (8:12; 9:39; 12:46). Hence we again find that the expression "from darkness to light" conjures up a New Testament perspective on conversion.

Central to the discontinuity brought about by spiritual birth is the relationship between the believer and Jesus. That belief in Jesus is necessary is underscored in the second part of the discourse delivered to Nicodemus (vv. 11–21). God has sent Jesus so that those who believe in him may have life and salvation. Later discourses describe at length the close character of the relationship between Jesus and those who believe in him. Believers are branches, and Jesus is the vine (15:1–7). As the world hates Jesus, so it must hate his followers (15:18–19). The father has given believers into Jesus' care, and they belong to him (17:6–10). To be born spiritually is to belong to Jesus.

Finally, birth "from above" means that one receives a new spirit. Just as there is breath or wind *(pneuma)* at physical birth, there is breath or spirit *(pneuma)* given in the second birth. To be *ek tou pneumatos,* from the Spirit, is to receive a new spirit as do the disciples after the resurrection of Jesus (20:22; cf. 7:39).[13]

All three aspects of new birth (discontinuity, relationship to Jesus, new spirit) come as the result of God's action. Jesus repeatedly claims that it is God who has sent him and to whom he will return (e.g., 3:16–17; 5:23, 37; 14:1–4). Similarly, believers are *not* reborn of their own volition but as the result of God's initiative.

At this point, the Johannine understanding of being born from above might seem to be just the kind of private, individualistic religious experience that is today often equated with born-again language. There are, however, some implications in John that distinguish the two points of view. John's notion is accompanied by both an emphasis on the corporate character of Christian faith and an interest in the ethical dimension of faith.

The corporate character of faith is not absent even in what appears to be a private discussion between Jesus and Nicodemus. The reference to the water of baptism in v. 5 already suggests that the one who is "born from above" is born into the community of the baptized. The connection between new birth and baptism is underscored by the story immediately following this discourse, in which Jesus himself baptizes (3:22).

That this kind of birth is not a private act but one with a corporate dimension finds confirmation in Jesus' words to Nicodemus in 3:7: "You must be born from above" [au. trans.]. The "you" in the Greek text, however, is *plural* rather than *singular*. The Johannine Jesus does not claim that Nicodemus alone must be born again, but that all must be born anew, that is, from above.

John does not convey this corporate dimension of spiritual birth through descriptions of the church's activity, as does Luke, nor through discussions of the body of Christ, as does Paul. That fact does not, however, mean that John has no concept of church or community.[14] The later discourses carefully weave together the fellowship of those who believe in Jesus (15:1–11). Just as they belong to him, they also belong to one another (15:12; 17:18–22). The later Johannine epistles make abundant use of this motif in order to combat enemies of the community (1 John 3:11; 4:7–21). While individual believers are newly born through their faith in Jesus, those believers are also born into fellowship with one another. New birth and new life are not simply private experiences.

It is also inaccurate to exclude the ethical dimension from John's use of the language of new birth and new life. The dualism that allows John to make a sharp distinction between those who have new life and those who do not also has an ethical component, as is clear already at the end of the discourse in John 3:19–21:[15]

> And this is the judgment, that the light has come into the world, and men loved darkness rather than light, because their deeds were evil. For every one who does evil hates the light, and does not come to the light, lest his deeds should be exposed. But he who does what is true comes to the light, that it may be clearly seen that his deeds have been wrought in God.

The one who is born spiritually is characterized by deeds that may see the light, deeds done through God. One's actions will be consistent with one's position. Those who belong to Jesus will behave in a way that produces good fruit (15:1–12).

The importance of ethical behavior becomes a major concern for the writer of the Johannine epistles, who connects this behavior with new birth:

> If you know that he [Jesus] is righteous, you may be sure that every one who does right is born of him. (1 John 2:29)

> No one born of God commits sin; for God's nature abides in him, and he cannot sin because he is born of God. By this it may be seen who are the children of God, and who are the children of the devil: whoever does not do right is not of God, nor he who does not love his brother. (1 John 3: 9–10)

There is a perfectionistic strand here insofar as the writer claims that the one born of God *cannot* sin. That claim needs to be compared with an earlier statement in the same letter which offers comfort for those who *do* sin (1 John 2:1–2). It seems that the writer is caught between the knowledge that believers do sin and the conviction that those who have received new life belong to God in such a direct and intense way that they ought not even be able to sin.[16] Thus, the claim of 1 John 3:2 may offer a more balanced representation of the writer's view:

> Beloved, we are God's children now; it does not yet appear what we shall be, but we know that when he appears we shall be like him, for we shall see him as he is.

Language of new birth as shaped in the Gospel of John and developed in the epistles describes a radical change in the life of a person who believes in Jesus. There is a sharp discontinuity involved in the birth in that it breaks the person's ties to "this world" and its perceptions. In the new life the individual lives in close relationship to Jesus and is possessed of a new spirit. While new birth occurs for individuals, it also has a corporate dimension. By virtue of the individual's relationship with Jesus, a relationship exists with others who have been born from above, and a new community emerges. This new community is characterized by its love of God and also by its love for others. Birth from above gives one a renewed understanding of what God demands from human beings and thus the one born spiritually is born ethically as well.

1 PETER

Immediately following the opening salutation in 1 Peter, we find this in 1 Pet. 1:3–5:

> Blessed be the God and Father of our Lord Jesus Christ! By his great mercy *we have been born anew [anagennēsas]* to a living hope through the resurrection of Jesus Christ from the dead, and to an inheritance which is imperishable, undefiled, and unfading, kept in heaven for you, who by God's power are guarded through faith for a salvation ready to be revealed in the last time.

This notion of the new birth of believers recurs throughout the early part of the letter. In 1:14, the recipients of the letter are exhorted "as obedient children" and in 2:2 "like newborn babes." Again in 1:23 we find, "You have been born anew, not of perishable seed but of imperishable, through the living and abiding word of God." While John's story of Nicodemus is admittedly the best-known reference to birth "from above" or spiritual birth, 1 Peter contains more extensive usage of this imagery.

Because of its location at the outset of the letter, 1 Pet. 1:3–5 warrants exploration. A more literal translation of this passage than the above, which was taken from the RSV, will provide a useful starting point:

> Blessed [be] the God and Father of our Lord Jesus Christ, who according to his great mercy caused us to be born anew into a living hope through the resurrection of Jesus Christ from the dead, into an imperishable and undefiled and unfading inheritance which has been kept in heaven for you, who have been guarded by the power of God through faith into a salvation that is ready to be revealed in the last age. (au. trans.)

This translation makes for an awkward and lengthy English sentence, but that is unavoidable if we are to do justice to the fact that in Greek—by contrast with several modern translations—all of the above comes in one sentence. The new birth of believers is not a topic separate from the praise of God, but is one of the reasons for the praise of God.

God is praised because *God* "caused us to be born anew." Unlike the RSV's *"we* have been born anew," which suggests some action or initiative on the part of believers, the Greek describes God as the one who *causes* or *gives* birth.[17] The expression used here for new birth is not that which is used in John 3, *gennasthai anōthen* (to be born from above), but is *anagennasthai* (to be born anew). It appears in the New Testament only here and in 1:23.

Two prepositional phrases, "according to his great mercy" and "through the resurrection of Jesus Christ," illumine the cause of the new birth of believers. Reference to God's mercy frequently appears in blessings such as this one.[18] In addition, the writer later characterizes the change in his audience as a movement from "not having received mercy" to "having received mercy" (2:10, au. trans.). To be born anew is possible only by the mercy of God.

Further, new birth occurs through or by means of the resurrection of Jesus. Jesus' resurrection does not magically provide access to rebirth. Instead, the resurrection certifies that the God who raised

Jesus may be trusted (1:21). The resurrection, which is God's action, creates the opportunity for forgiveness (3:18–22) and faith.

Two additional prepositional phrases in vv. 3–5 clarify the result of the believer's new birth, "to a living hope" and "to an inheritance . . ."[19] New birth does not provide a new life, which might be construed as a private experience, but a new and living hope.[20] That the hope mentioned here is not a wish or desire but an expectation (1:13; 3:15), a guarantee, becomes clear in the second prepositional phrase. New birth moves one into "an imperishable and undefiled and unfading inheritance." Pressing the analogy of new birth to include a new inheritance, the author describes an inheritance that can never be used up and which is assured ("kept in heaven for you, who have been guarded by the power of God"). Both the new children and the inheritance are protected from harm until the right time comes. God is blessed then, not only for giving new birth, but also for providing for those who are born from above.

Because other references to new birth (1:14, 23; 2:2) and additional instances of conversion language (2:9–10; 2:25) follow this opening blessing, students of 1 Peter have often suggested that it contains an early baptismal homily or baptismal liturgy. On this reading of the letter, the extensive ethical teachings appear in order to provide instructions for new converts. References to persecution (e.g., 1:6; 2:20–21; 3:13–17; 5:10) are understood to occupy only a secondary place in the letter.[21]

This reconstruction of the origin of 1 Peter is attractive at first glance, especially when attention is being given to the language of new birth and new life. Upon closer examination, however, it becomes clear that there is insufficient evidence to support the reconstruction. To begin with, explicit reference to baptism appears only once in the letter (3:21). While it is easy to imagine that new birth was understood to occur at baptism, and while the two are connected elsewhere in early Christianity, 1 Peter does not directly connect the two.[22] Indeed, the expressions "God . . . caused us to be born anew" (1:3) and "we have been born anew" (1:23) are in the aorist or past tense, not the present, which one would expect from material that addressed those being baptized.[23]

For these reasons and others, the origin of 1 Peter must be sought elsewhere. Several commentators have argued that 1 Peter comes from a context of some kind of persecution.[24] The recent investigations of David Balch and John Elliott tend to confirm that hypothesis. Balch investigates the household code of 1 Pet. 2:11—3:12 by drawing on the Greco-Roman philosophical tradition, in which orders of domestic subordination were established. Like other minority religious groups, Christians had been charged with undermining this set of social assumptions, and the author of 1 Peter presents the code as a way of defending Christians against claims that they were antisocial.[25]

John Elliott argues that the audience of 1 Peter consists not of those who were "exiles" spiritually, but of those who were in fact "resident aliens" and "visiting strangers," people who were geographically and socially dislocated. Because these homeless Christians experienced great social tension, they found conformity with the larger Gentile society an attractive option. In response to this situation, the writer of 1 Peter reminds his audience that they do have "a distinctive communal identity" which requires "discipline and cohesion" within and "separation from Gentile influences without."[26]

Although their conclusions are at odds with one another in that Balch sees a community that increasingly adjusts itself to outside expectations and Elliott one that separates itself from the mainstream, Balch and Elliott concur that persecution in the form of social pressure and conflict shapes the letter of 1 Peter.[27] The concern with persecution that runs throughout the letter does not mean that a legal, official persecution is underway, but it may well reflect extreme tension between Christians and their neighbors.

This conclusion helps us to assess more adequately the new birth language in 1 Peter. If Balch and Elliott have correctly identified a situation of social tension and persecution behind 1 Peter, then the language of new birth plays a significant role in the boundary-setting purpose of the letter. Especially in Elliott's reading of the letter, one major task of the letter is to establish the boundary of the community, thereby strengthening its identity in the face of persecution. Those who are on the outside are not to set standards for believers, but believers are to identify with one another. Several ways of referring to the boundary of the believing community appear in the letter. It is a chosen race (2:9), the household of God (4:17), the flock of God (5:2). It is also the collection of those whom God has caused to be born again (1:3), because the imagery of new birth and new life refers not merely to the moment of conversion but also to "the termination of previous social ties and the commencement of new associations."[28] New birth moves the believer within the boundaries of the new community.

Theologically, new birth language in 1 Peter has to do with soteriology. Salvation belongs to those to whom God has given new birth. It *belongs* as an assured promise for the future, however, not as a fully realized gift in the present (1:5; 1:13; 2:2). Those who have been born from above know who is the author of their salvation, but they do not themselves possess that salvation. Instead, they are able to grow into it:

> Like newborn babes, long for the pure spiritual milk, that by it you may grow up to salvation; for you have tasted the kindness of the Lord. (2:2–3)

The claim that new believers "grow up to salvation" or, more literally, "grow unto" or "grow in" salvation, means that they mature into full possession of what is already theirs. New birth involves assurance that even persecution and suffering do not deprive the believer of God's glory, strength, and comfort (5:10).

In addition to having soteriological import, new birth imagery has ethical implications:

> As obedient children, do not be conformed to the passions of your former ignorance, but as he who called you is holy, be holy yourselves in all your conduct. . . . (1:14–15)

> Having purified your souls by obedience to the truth for a sincere love of the brethren, love one another earnestly from the heart. You have been born anew *(anagegennēmenoi),* not of perishable seed but of imperishable, through the living and abiding word of God. (1:22–23)

The boundary that one crosses at new birth has ethical as well as social and soteriological implications. The believer receives a heart and mind that are capable of holiness. The ethical instruction of this letter does not appear at the end as the letter's "conclusion," but is interwoven because new birth is not only a spiritual but also an ethical category.

Imagery of new birth in 1 Peter is a part of the letter's general task of assisting the audience to see within its fellowship a household with an identity distinct from that of the larger culture. In this context the language of conversion applies not simply to an individual but to the individual's "birth" into a new home. To be born anew, then, is to enter a new society which has its origin and result in God and which is thereby enabled to live hopefully in a perilous social setting.

CONCLUSIONS

While there are great differences between 1 Peter and the Gospel of John, the two use the motif of new birth in similar ways. For each, new birth signals discontinuity that is ethical, social or communal, and soteriological. As 1 Peter urges believers to "be holy" (1 Peter 1:14–15), John follows the words of Jesus about birth "from above" with the claim that those who are so born act in accordance with light rather than darkness (John 3:19–21). The call for birth "from above" in John's Gospel is issued to a community ("you [plural] must be born anew") in which there exists mutual love and solidarity (John 15:1–12; 17:18–22). 1 Peter similarly employs the notion of new birth to call believers to an identity apart from the surrounding culture. In both writers, the soteriological dimension of discontinuity rings loudly. To enter the kingdom requires birth from above (John); the birth God has given is salvation (1 Peter).

This rich use of "birth from above" language is a far cry from contemporary usage in which to be "born again" is to enter into a personal, even individualistic, relationship with Jesus. The writers of the Fourth Gospel and of 1 Peter would have found it odd to hear people describe themselves as "born again" apart from a "born from above" manner of living and a "born of the Spirit" community. For them, birth in Christ is a beginning, not an ending.

NOTES

1. Titus 3:5 also speaks of God who "saved us, not because of deeds done by us in righteousness, but in virtue of his own mercy, *by the washing of regeneration* and renewal in the Holy Spirit. . . ."

The Synoptic tradition contains a saying that may be related to John 3:3: "Whoever does not receive the kingdom of heaven like a child shall not enter it" (Mark 10:15; cf. Matt. 18:3; Luke 18:17). On the possible connection between the two, see R. E. Brown, *The Gospel According to John I–XII* (Garden City, N.Y.: Doubleday & Co., 1966), 143–44.

2. Brown, *John I–XII*, 139. See also, E. G. Selwyn, *The First Epistle of St. Peter* (London: Macmillan & Co., 1947), 122–23.

3. C. H. Dodd, *The Interpretation of the Fourth Gospel* (Cambridge: At the Univ. Press, 1970), 303. See also C. K. Barrett, *The Gospel According to St. John,* 2d ed. (Philadelphia: Westminster Press, 1978), 204; Severino Pancaro, *The Law in the Fourth Gospel* (Leiden: E. J. Brill, 1975), 86; Ernst Haenchen, *The Gospel of John,* trans. R. W. Funk (Philadelphia: Fortress Press, 1984), 1:200.

4. Rudolf Schnackenburg, *The Gospel According to St. John,* trans. K. Smyth (New York: Herder & Herder, 1968), 1:363.

5. Brown, *John I–XII,* 129.

6. J. L. Martyn, *History and Theology in the Fourth Gospel,* 2d ed. (Nashville: Abingdon Press, 1979).

7. I cannot agree with Schnackenburg's judgment that *anōthen* can only be translated here as "from above" (*Gospel According to John,* 1:366–68). While it is clear that Jesus' saying is to be heard as "birth from above," nevertheless the misunderstanding of Nicodemus depends on the double meaning of *anōthen* (see Brown, *John I–XII,* 130–31; R. Alan Culpepper, *Anatomy of the Fourth Gospel: A Study in Literary Design* [Philadelphia: Fortress Press, 1983], 155).

8. Brown, *John I–XII,* cxxxv, 130–31, 138–41. See also the discussion of R. Alan Culpepper in *Anatomy of the Fourth Gospel,* 152–65.

9. Brown, *John I–XII,* 141–44; Schnackenburg, *John,* 370–71; Haenchen, *John,* 200–201.

10. It is sometimes argued that "of water" is a late insertion into the Gospel, but there is no manuscript evidence for deleting "of water." For the arguments, see Brown, *John I–XII,* 142–44, and Schnackenburg, *John,* 369.

11. Already in the postexilic period the theme of being begotten as God's children exists, though not extensively. See above, 130–31.

12. Rudolf Bultmann, *The Gospel of John* (Philadelphia: Westminster Press, 1971), 137; Barrett, *John,* 206.

13. A. R. C. Leaney, "The Johannine Paraclete and the Qumran Scrolls," *John and Qumran,* ed. J. H. Charlesworth (London: Geoffrey Chapman, 1972), 51; Brown, *John I–XII,* 140.

14. On this, see Brown, *John I–XII,* cviii–cix; and John F. O'Grady, *Individual and Community in John* (Rome: Pontifical Biblical Institute, 1978).

15. The literature on Johannine dualism is extensive. For a review of the issues, consult Robert Kysar, *The Fourth Evangelist and His Gospel: An Examination of Contemporary Scholarship* (Minneapolis: Augsburg Pub. House, 1975), 131–36, 215–21.

16. For an explanation of the many attempts at unraveling this contradiction, see R. E. Brown, *The Epistles of John* (Garden City, N.Y.: Doubleday & Co., 1982), 412–16.

17. Compare the Jerusalem Bible, "[God] has given us a new birth," and the New English Bible, "[God] gave us new birth."

18. E.g., 2 Cor. 1:3. See Victor Paul Furnish, "Elect Sojourners in Christ: An Approach to the Theology of I Peter," *Perkins Journal* 28 (1975):7.

19. Ibid., 8.

20. So Norbert Brox, *Der erste Petrusbrief* (Zurich: Benziger Verlag, 1979), 61. But see also Friedrich Büchsel (*"anagennaō," TDNT*, 2:673), who claims that hope here is only "a personal attitude."

21. For a concise survey of the literature, see David L. Balch, *Let Wives Be Submissive: The Domestic Code in I Peter* (Chico, Calif.: Scholars Press, 1981), 1–20.

22. Selwyn concludes that "the evidence does not enable us to decide" whether 1 Peter intended to refer directly to baptism (*First Epistle of St. Peter,* 123). J. N. D. Kelly comments that the baptismal note in 1 Pet. 1:3–5 is "unmistakable," but as evidence he offers Titus 3:5–7, Rom. 8:14–24, Col. 3:1–4, and 1 John 2:29—3:2. Of these, only Titus 3:5–7 refers to baptism ("the washing of regeneration") and that in no way requires the conclusion that 1 Pet. 1:3–5 also refers to baptism (*A Commentary on the Epistles of Peter and of Jude* [New York: Harper & Row, 1969], 46).

23. John H. Elliott, *The Elect and the Holy: An Exegetical Examination of 1 Peter 2:4–10 and the Phrase* basileion hierateuma (Leiden: E. J. Brill, 1966), 165.

24. Balch, *Let Wives Be Submissive,* 10–14.

25. Ibid., 81–121.

26. John H. Elliott, *A Home for the Homeless: A Sociological Exegesis of I Peter, Its Situation and Strategy* (Philadelphia: Fortress Press, 1981), esp. 148.

27. For a comparison of the two, see Antoinette Wire's review essay in *RSR* 10 (1984): 209–16.

28. Elliott, *Home for the Homeless,* 119.

Conclusion

In the preceding chapters we have explored conversion narratives and imagery in a variety of New Testament texts. Here I want to reflect on the implications of this study for contemporary understandings of conversion. In order to do that, we need to bear in mind the kinds of questions we have—and have not—addressed.

To begin with, there has been no attempt here at a comprehensive description of conversion in the New Testament. Such a description might have included a study of the ministry of John the Baptist, Jesus' call to repentance, or the parables of Jesus. Arguably, each of the above has to do with a kind of conversion, but in none of these cases is conversion an explicit feature of the text. Neither has there been an attempt to track the social pattern of conversion in the earliest Christian communities. The question of *who* converted to Christianity is receiving great attention elsewhere,[1] and, while it has enormous significance for our reading of the texts, as we saw in 1 Peter, it is a separate and distinct issue from those addressed here. We have also not dwelt on the similarities and differences between conversion in early Christianity and conversion in other Greco-Roman religions, since the evidence involved in that study would come largely from post-New Testament texts.[2]

The primary task of this study has been a literary-theological probe of major New Testament narratives of conversion and images of conversion, with particular attention to texts that have given rise to contemporary conversion language. The controlling question has been how the text portrays conversion, not how the *converted* see their own conversions, except as the authors of the texts may be reflecting on their own conversions. Here, as often, we are limited by our own sources. We do not know what the "typical" Christian of the first century believed or felt or thought. Instead, the goal has been to learn what understandings of conversion are reflected in the texts.

SUMMARY

Paul, as indicated in chapter 1, seldom uses conventional language of conversion. Behind the varied expressions that he does employ stands the conviction that conversion is the individual's response to the *apocalypse* of Jesus Christ. Paul had himself been forced by the *apocalypse* to see that Jesus was God's Messiah and to revise radically his own previous commitments (Gal. 1:11–17; Phil. 3:2–11). This transformation he understood to be definitive of Christian existence (Rom. 12:1–2). All believers, by virtue of their baptism into Christ, experience a radical change in perception (Gal. 3:23–28).

Luke's inclusion of a variety of conversion narratives, especially in Acts 8—11, serves his description of the expanding boundaries of the church. The story of the Ethiopian eunuch, a mysterious figure who represents the extremes of the known world, foreshadows the movement of the gospel into the "end of the earth" (Acts 1:8). Paul's reversal signals the power of God's church even over its enemies. The inclusion of Cornelius signals the overthrow of traditional barriers and the beginning of the Gentile mission. Luke does not offer a concept or theory of conversion, but a changing portrait with certain constant features. In these texts, conversion is always initiated by God. Conversion has to do with individuals, but it also incorporates those individuals into the larger community. Conversion is not an end in itself but, in Luke's stories, it is a beginning.

In the Gospel of John and in 1 Peter, conversion requires a sharp discontinuity between past and present, which results in the birth of the believer "from above." The one who is so born receives a new spirit and enters into a close relationship with Jesus, expressed in John through various images. 1 Peter employs the discontinuity of conversion in order to argue for the clarification of the community's boundaries. Those who are converted exist together in hope, distinct from those on the outside.

In my introduction, I argued for the development of a typology of conversion, and it will enhance this overview to return to that issue. One chronic difficulty that accompanies discussions of conversion is that many different and conflicting definitions of conversion are employed. For some, the term conversion applies only to a sudden and radical change of conviction. Others use the word for any change in affiliation. Behind this confusion stands the fact that change occurs in many different ways and that no one pattern can be described as "real" or "genuine" conversion. Instead of attempting to restrict the term to one type of change, I argued that there are (at least) three types of conversion: *alternation, pendulum-like conversion*, and *transformation*. Alternation occurs when change grows out of an individual's past behavior. It is the logical consequence of previous choices. Pendulum conversion involves the rejection of past convictions and affiliations for an affirmed present and future. Transformation applies to conversions in which a new way of perception forces the radical reinterpretation of the past. Here the past is not rejected but reconstrued as part of a new understanding of God and world.

Each of these types of conversion appears in the pages of the New Testament. In Luke's narrative of the emerging church, he describes the *alternations* of the Ethiopian eunuch and of Cornelius. When the eunuch appears in Acts 8, he has been worshiping in Jerusalem and is reading from Isaiah. His eagerness to speak with Philip suggests a search for understanding, which is rewarded in his baptism. His conversion requires no rejection of past thought or action. Instead, the eunuch's conversion comes as a logical consequence of earlier choices. Similarly, the centurion Cornelius was a "devout man who feared God with all his household, gave alms liberally to the people, and prayed constantly to God" (10:2). His angelic visitor tells him that God has remembered his deeds (10:4), implying that the conversion of Cornelius comes in recognition of his previously established faithfulness. Although the alternations of the eunuch and of Cornelius have great significance for the church and cause upheaval within the church, the subjects of these events appear to go through only a natural development. Indeed, part of the impact of these stories lies in the conflict between the obvious worthiness of the converts and the shock caused by their identities as outsiders.

Pendulum conversion also appears in Luke's second volume, in the first account of Paul's conversion. According to Acts 9, Paul swings from violent opponent of the church to its loyal disciple. He comes on the scene in Acts 8 as the fulfillment of Stephen's words about Israel's persecution of its prophets. When he exits in Acts 9, he has begun to proclaim the gospel *and* to be persecuted. While it would be inaccurate to call this a conversion from Judaism to Christianity, it does represent a reversal in Paul's activity.

Another example of pendulum conversion occurs in the imagery of birth from above and new life found in the Gospel of John and in 1 Peter. Fed by dualism, this imagery portrays a sharp break between the believer's life in Christ and past life. To be born from above or to be born anew is to be separated from one's earlier life. Past associations and convictions are rejected when new ones are formed. The dichotomy in language is that of pendulum conversion, in which past and present are disconnected.

In the letters of Paul, we see a more complex relationship between the believer's past and present. Here the past is not rejected but reinterpreted; it takes on a different meaning because of a new set of circumstances. When Paul comments about his reception of the gospel in Galatians 1 and Philippians 3, he describes himself as one whose convictions have been transformed. By virtue of revelation (Gal. 1:11–12), he came to see that Jesus was indeed Messiah *and* that his own accomplishments amounted to nothing. Paul does not cut himself off from his past life. Romans 9:1–5 indicates a continued and strong tie with his fellow Jews, which must be taken into account. The *apocalypse* of Jesus Christ does not require the rejection of the past, but its reinterpretation—its transformation.

ISSUES FOR CONTEMPORARY DISCUSSION

Discovery of these varied types and varied understandings of conversion in the New Testament presents us with a number of issues for ongoing discussion. A critical question to be addressed to mainline denominations, at least in North America, is whether they have adequately explored the neaning of conversion. Many "liberal" Christians have tended to associate discussion of conversion with pietism or with evangelical Christianity. Particularly because of the excesses of some missionary movements, liberal Christians have avoided the task of understanding and reflecting upon conversion. Even the use of the term has been abdicated in some quarters. Surely this posture discards baby along with bathwater. If the category of conversion has been misused and misunderstood, then liberal Christians are obliged to develop a view of conversion rather than flee the task out of embarrassment.[3]

The question of conversion does not occupy a peripheral place in the New Testament. Although the New Testament texts are not missionary texts, designed to convert their readers and hearers, they are written for converts. Integral to these texts is the problem of defining Christian faith, which includes the question of Christian identity, the defining of Christian life, and the constituting of Christian community. Since these are the very questions that also plague—and ought to plague—beleaguered mainline Christianity today, they must not be ignored.

To be sure, there are forms of present-day Christianity that place great emphasis on the personal conversion experience. Much of the energy in these Christian communities is directed toward church growth and personal evangelism. Our study results in some critical questions for Christians who operate out of this perspective.

First we need to ask whether the emphasis on a personal conversion experience makes conversion into a goal, an end in itself. Certainly, to interpret the work of the church as the "winning of souls" or the "evangelization of the world" is to make conversion into a final product. That attitude flatly contradicts what we have seen in the New Testament, where conversion is discussed as a byproduct of the gospel. Not even in Acts do the well-known stories of conversion appear in order to show *how* people are won or *how* the church operates. The stories illustrate God's action—at times even in spite of the church (e.g., Acts 9:13–14; 10:9–16).

Another issue for those who would insist on the personal conversion experience is whether they have adequately taken into account the ethical dimension of conversion. Often conversion is described essentially as a religious or sentimental experience that brings one into relationship with Jesus. While our texts admittedly understand conversion as involving a relationship with Jesus, that relationship is not a sentimental one. It does not center on an adoration of the life of Jesus or even on awe of the powerful deeds of Jesus. Instead, conversion in the New Testament requires the acknowledgment that Jesus is the obedient and chosen Messiah of God, and that acknowledgment in turn requires a life of obedience.

Similarly, conversion in the texts we have studied does not pertain merely to an individual's act of conviction and commitment. Conversion moves the individual believer into the community of believers. Even Luke's stories of the dramatic conversions of the eunuch, Paul, and Cornelius connect those individuals with the larger church. In light of this, the emphasis on personal evangelism in some quarters of the Christian community needs to be reexamined. A profession of faith without partnership in the community means very little.

For contemporary Christians of all persuasions, it may be difficult to acknowledge the overwhelming extent to which our texts represent conversion as an act of God. Paul speaks of being called by God (Gal. 1:15–17) and exhorts believers to allow themselves to be transformed (Rom. 12:1–2). Luke attributes even small details in the conversion narratives to the will or plan of God. God, or God's agent, sends Philip, Ananias, and Peter. 1 Peter describes God as the one who "caused us to be born anew." To modern ears, accustomed to the notion of human freedom and responsibility, this constant reference to the action of God creates confusion and discomfort. Are we merely puppets who are manipulated by God?

We can unravel this problem only by recalling the nature of the texts involved. None of the writers of the New Testament were concerned with the systematic issue of the relationship between human and divine freedom and power. Thus, when Luke writes that God sent Peter to Cornelius, he does not at the same time mean that Cornelius and Peter lack freedom. Luke is concerned, rather, with reminding his own community that God has been with them all along and that God has directed the expansion of the church. The claim that God is powerful is, in this context, a pastoral statement more than a systematic philosophical proposition.

The emphasis on God's initiative needs to be understood also as an aspect of God's grace. When Luke says that God chose the Ethiopian eunuch or Paul or Cornelius or anyone else, he does not view that selection as a display of power designed to convey the convert's weakness, but as a display of God's grace. Again in Paul's letters we see that God's initiative derives from grace rather than from some self-serving desire merely to demonstrate power.

A final issue that challenges contemporary Christians to further reflection is the way in which New Testament texts assume that conversion involves a real—even a radical—change in the life of the believer. This conviction runs throughout the texts we have studied and others we have barely touched. Conversion brings new life (John 3:1–7), a transformed mind (Rom. 12:1–2), a new community (Acts 11:1–18), a new perspective (Phil. 3:2–11). Can it be said that contemporary Christianity either believes or proclaims that conversion means real change in the believer's perspective and actions? Until we do believe, proclaim, and embody that change in the way we live as individuals and as communities, we have not understood what it means to move from "darkness to light."

NOTES

1. See, for example, Gerd Theissen, *The Social Setting of Pauline Christianity: Essays on Corinth,* trans. & ed. John H. Schütz (Philadelphia: Fortress Press, 1982), 69–119; Malherbe, *Social Aspects of Early Christianity,* 29–59; Wayne A. Meeks, *The First Urban Christians: The Social World of the Apostle Paul* (New Haven, Conn.: Yale Univ. Press, 1983), 51–73.

2. On these questions consult the classic work of A. D. Nock, *Conversion: The Old and New in Religion from Alexander the Great to Augustine of Hippo* (London: Oxford Univ. Press, 1933); and Ramsay MacMullen, *Christianizing the Roman Empire* (New Haven, Conn.: Yale Univ. Press, 1984).

3. Some important contributions to this effort appear in David C. Steinmetz, "Reformation and Conversion," *Theology Today* 35 (1978): 25–32; and in Thomas Groome, "Conversion, Nurture and Educators," *Religious Education* 76 (1981): 482–96.

Suggestions

for Further Reading

Beker, J. Christiaan. *Paul the Apostle: The Triumph of God in Life and Thought.* Philadelphia: Fortress Press, 1980. A seminal treatment of Paul's thought. While Beker regards the category of conversion as an inappropriate entry into Paul's thought, he eventually concedes the need to give an account of the function and meaning of Paul's call.

Conn, Walter, ed. *Conversion: Perspectives on Personal and Social Transformation.* New York: Alba House, 1978. This collection of essays from the perspectives of history, psychology, and theology provides an excellent introduction to contemporary discussion. Special attention is given to conversion as a process of integration and to its implications for social change.

Crampsey, James A. *The Conversion of Cornelius (Acts 10:1—11:18): Societal Apologetic and Ecclesial Tension.* Ann Arbor, Mich.: University Microfilms No. 9995571, 1982. An exploration of the Cornelius account in the contexts of Greco-Roman conversions and of Lukan conversion stories.

Dibelius, Martin. *Studies in the Acts of the Apostles.* New York: Charles Scribner's Sons; London: SCM Press, 1956. Dibelius's essay on the conversion of Cornelius has largely determined discussions of that story for three decades.

Dupont, Jacques, O.S.B. *The Salvation of the Gentiles: Studies in the Acts of the Apostles.* New York: Paulist Press, 1979. Included in these studies is an essay on conversion in Acts, which argues that for Luke conversion requires a "sense of sinfulness," an understanding of God's mystery, and a change of life.

Gaventa, Beverly Roberts. *Paul's Conversion: A Critical Sifting of the Epistolary Evidence.* Ann Arbor, Mich.: University Microfilms No. 7905353, 1978. An examination of the texts in Paul's letters that refer to his conversion; includes a review of research on Paul's conversion.

James, William. *The Varieties of Religious Experience: A Study in Human Nature.* London: Longmans, Green & Co., 1902. James's lectures on the divided self and on conversion provide the acknowledged starting point for discussion on the psychology of conversion.

Kerr, Hugh T. and John Mulder, eds. *Conversions: The Christian Experience.* Grand Rapids: Wm. B. Eerdmans, 1983. A convenient gathering of prominent stories of conversion, from Paul to Charles Colson, with brief introductions to each account.

Kim, Seyoon. *The Origin of Paul's Gospel.* Grand Rapids: Wm. B. Eerdmans, 1982. Drawing on both Paul's letters and Acts, Kim argues that Paul received the content of the gospel he preached in the Christophany on the Damascus road.

Lohfink, Gerhard. *The Conversion of St. Paul: Narrative and History in Acts.* Chicago: Franciscan Herald Press, 1976. Written for a general audience, this volume sets the problem of the three Acts accounts in the context of traditional and contemporary biblical scholarship.

MacMullen, Ramsay. *Christianizing the Roman Empire: A.D. 100–400.* New Haven, Conn.: Yale Univ. Press, 1984. An engaging study of the rise of Christianity as it might have appeared to prospective converts.

Munck, Johannes. *Paul and the Salvation of Mankind.* Richmond: John Knox Press, 1959. Munck's initial chapter argues that both the letters of Paul and the stories of Acts describe his call in language reminiscent of prophetic calls in the Old Testament.

Nock, Arthur Darby. *Conversion: The Old and New in Religion from Alexander the Great to Augustine of Hippo.* London: Oxford Univ. Press, 1933. After half a century, this study of conversion to Christianity in the context of Greco-Roman religion remains a valuable resource.

Rambo, Lewis. "Current Research on Religious Conversion." *Religious Studies Review* 8 (1982):145–59. An extensive bibliography of works on conversion in anthropology, sociology, history, psychology, and theology.

Stendahl, Krister. *Paul Among Jews and Gentiles and Other Essays.* Philadelphia: Fortress Press, 1976. In "Call Rather Than Conversion" Stendahl maintains that Paul does not have a conversion, a change of religions, but a call.

Wallis, Jim. *The Call to Conversion: Recovering the Gospel for These Times.* San Francisco: Harper & Row, 1981. An impassioned plea for Christian transformation that issues in commitment to a new world order and an altered life style for believers.

Index of Passages

SCRIPTURE

155

APOCRYPHA AND PSEUDEPIGRAPHA

OTHER ANCIENT TEXTS